AMERICA AND THE FOUR JAPANS

America

and _the_ Four

Frederik L. Schodt

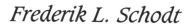

Japans

friend
foe
model
mirror

Stone Bridge Press
Berkeley, California

Other books by Frederik L. Schodt

Inside the Robot Kingdom:
Japan, Mechatronics, and the Coming Robotopia
Manga! Manga! The World of Japanese Comics

Published by STONE BRIDGE PRESS
P.O. Box 8208, Berkeley, California 94707
TEL 510-524-8732 / FAX 510-524-8711

LIBRARY OF CONGRESS CATALOGING-IN-PUBLICATION DATA

Schodt, Frederik L.
    America and the four Japans: friend, foe, model, mirror /
    Frederik L. Schodt.
        p.   cm.
    Includes bibliographical references and index.
    ISBN 1-880656-10-8 (pbk.)—ISBN 1-880656-06-X (bound).
    1. United States—Relations—Japan. 2. Japan—Relations—United
States.   I. Title.
E183.8.J3S34   1993
303.48'273052—dc20   93-31450
                                                          CIP

This book is dedicated to the memory
of Ranald MacDonald (A.D. 1824–1894)

CONTENTS

INTRODUCTION

No one ever tried harder than the American writer Lafcadio Hearn to understand Japan. Yet in 1891, a year after going to Japan to live there permanently, he wrote, "I am beginning to think I was a fool to write a book about Japan at all. My best consolation is that every year other people write books about Japan on the strength of a trip only;—and that excuse is very bad."[1]

For over a hundred and fifty years Americans, like Hearn, have been fascinated, even obsessed, with Japan. And in that time the Japan we have known has changed dramatically. First it was a quaint feudal nation. Then it became a small but rapidly modernizing Asian state, which quickly mushroomed into an empire and a mortal enemy. Then, almost overnight, it was transformed into a faithful ally and source of shoddy but inexpensive products. Now Japan is an economic and technological juggernaut, increasingly said to hold the key to our future. Not surprisingly, Americans have written hundreds, if not thousands of books about Japan in an attempt to understand it. But Japan remains shrouded in fog.

I believe it is as important to understand the different roles Japan plays in the American mind as it is to understand Japan itself. It is, after all, these roles—our *perceptions*—of Japan that define our relationship. They determine not only how we deal with Japan, but even how Japan behaves toward us. They create the reality. This book was therefore written as guide to, and a commentary on, four of these roles—on Japan as a friend, foe, model, and mirror.

The first half of this book is about how close Japan and America have become, and how far apart we remain, about the sources of our friendship and our conflicts. It is also an attempt to go back to the basics—to "square one"—and as such it includes some history as well as personal observations. The second half is about the rewards, problems, and pitfalls of trying to emulate Japan, as well as some of the ways Americans can use

Japan to better understand themselves. It contains more personal opinion, and speculation. Throughout, however, the goal is the same, and that is to explore the larger question of what Japan means to America.

As Hearn might have asked, What's my excuse for writing a book on Japan?

I first went to Japan in 1965 at the age of fifteen, and I have been deeply involved with Japan ever since. Today I live in the United States and proudly consider it my home in the true sense of the word, but I have an equal number of friends in both nations. For nearly twenty years I have been working with Japanese and American people not only as a writer, but as a professional translator and interpreter. As an interpreter, I have seen horrendous cultural misunderstandings and arguments, and near fist-fights erupt over matters both trivial and vital, and I have seen people who were convinced they did not like each other form fast friendships. As a translator, I been able to peer into slower written worlds where radically different logic and assumptions are employed, and to delight in the differences. This book is not about my own experiences. The opinions expressed, however, are based on them, and they are not those of someone from the world of business or academia or politics, but from the front lines of communications between Japan and America: from the trenches, if you will.

In recent years I have often met Americans who can micro-analyze Japan but know surprisingly little about the U.S.-Japan relationship itself. Yet to become involved with Japan—as more and more Americans are doing—is to enter into a very intimate relationship with a complicated history. I think it is important to know something about it. Even for old "Japan hands," it is important to periodically review how we got to where we are today.

In recent years I have also met many Americans who have read too many polemics—books on Japan written by either harsh critics or fawning admirers. I have never felt comfortable with this dualism. I believe there is a need for more concise, straightforward works that keep to the middle of the road. In this book I have therefore made a point of looking at the big picture and focusing on basic commonalities and differences.

It might seem odd that I concentrate almost exclusively on Japan and America and rarely use the broader terms "East" or "West." Why, in this age of interdependence, do I so ignore the rest of the world?

The first answer is that for both economic and political reasons the relationship between Japan and America has become terribly important to the health of the whole world today; simultaneously, the Japan-U.S. connection offers the possibility of global good and global catastrophe.

Second, use of the words "East" or "West" is a legacy of a time long past, when most Americans lived physically in the New World but mentally in Europe, where Japan has always been to the "East" because that is the direction people first traveled to get there. To Americans, however, Japan is to the "West," and it is time for us to think on our own, to find a non-Eurocentric view of our Pacific neighbor.

It was hard to write knowledgeably and well about Japan in Lafcadio Hearn's day, and it may be even harder now. It involves walking down the same road so many others have while trying to observe the same scenery from a slightly different perspective. Like the United States, Japan is a highly dynamic and complex nation, an aggregate of millions of individuals with independent personalities and views. Making generalizations about Japan, therefore, becomes like tip-toeing through a minefield, trying to move forward in the right direction while avoiding the booby traps of irresponsibility.

This book is not intended to explain everything about Japan. What book could? Instead, I have strived for brevity and simplicity, and I hope that readers will be stimulated to explore further on their own. The information included here is as up-to-date as I could make it, but the discussion is designed to be more than just a snapshot of a single moment in the U.S.-Japan relationship. I have written this book mainly for Americans, which might include anyone in the New World, and if it helps even one person I will be happy, for in the process of writing I have learned a great deal myself.

Acknowledgments

I had assistance from a variety of sources, who all deserve profuse thanks. For suggesting "yet another" book on Japan, thanks go to my friend, editor, and publisher, Peter Goodman. For interviews, advice, and special assistance, thanks go to James N. Aliferis, Annie Apple-Mathews and Akira Nara, Jerome E. Barnett, Daigaku, Alan G. Gleason and Yuko Kitaura, Elizabeth Blish Hughes, Satoshi Kamata, Dan Kanagy, Leonard Koren, Raymond Larrett, Miyoko and Ami Mizuno, Shuichi Okada, Gary Rector, David W. Schodt, Eddie and Margie Schodt, Michihiro (Nikon) Shimabukuro, Keiko Tokioka, and Theodore Kusaburo Twine. Most of all, thanks to Misao, for her patience, encouragement, and support.

* * * * *

All translations of Japanese source material are by the author, unless otherwise indicated.

ONE

Friend

Alvah says that while guys like us are all excited about being real Orientals and wearing robes, actual Orientals over there are reading surrealism and Charles Darwin and mad about Western business suits. . . . Think what a great world revolution will take place when East meets West finally. . . .

Ray Smith to Jaffy Ryder before his trip to Japan,
in Jack Kerouac's *The Dharma Bums*, 1958

*A*ccording to geologists, America is moving west, in the general direction of Japan. It is a slow movement, the result of plate tectonics and continental drift, and amounts to only around two centimeters per year. But the attraction between Japan and the United States of America—the nations, not the land masses—is far more than geologic. On both an abstract and a real level our two nations have been growing closer at a dizzying pace.

When the United States declared independence in 1776, it consisted of thirteen states strung along the Atlantic coast of North America. Japan, which by then already had a long history, was a chain of islands floating off the eastern coast of mainland Asia. Both nations lay in nearly the same geographical orientation and latitude, yet were separated by nearly seven thousand miles as the crow flies. Actually getting from New York to Tokyo would have taken many months and required traveling over twenty thousand miles in a hazardous, roundabout voyage by sea. For most Americans, Japan might as well have been on another planet.

Extreme Isolation

Distance was not the only obstacle. In 1635, over 140 years before the United States was formed, Japan had adopted an extreme policy of isolation. Fearing European (particularly Portuguese and Spanish) encroachment and the divisive influence of Christianity, the ruling shogun had tried to seal off his country from the outside world. Save for limited trade conducted at the port of Nagasaki with the Dutch and Chinese, foreigners were not allowed in, and Japanese, if they left, were not allowed to return—on penalty of death.

The policy of isolation lasted over two hundred years. It gave Japan a long period of peace in which to fine-tune its social system and its arts and crafts, and it created much of what is distinctive about Japan today. But it also meant that Japan—which had been on a technological par with Europe except for navigation skills and guns—was cut off from the scientific fruits of the Renaissance and stuck in a feudal system far longer than it might have been otherwise. It did not mean that Japanese people were entirely ignorant of the outside world, however, or even of the New World.

Between 1543, when the Portuguese arrived in Japan, and the start of isolation in 1635, the Japanese had extensive contact with European traders and missionaries. And they were aggressive traders and settlers in their own right throughout Southeast Asia. In 1600, for example, the Philippines was a Spanish colony, but there was also a settlement of several thousand Japanese in Manila, and a few of them may even have worked as crews on galleons that sailed between the Philippines and Mexico. The first official recorded visit from Japan to the New World was in 1610, when the shogun sent some emissaries to Mexico on a Spanish galleon. Two years later, a mission of 183 merchants and samurai followed. Some traveled across Mexico all the way to Spain, while others remained in Acapulco and Mexico City for as long as six years. The voyage between Japan and Mexico alone took over ninety days.[1]

After the isolation policy began in 1635, news and knowledge of the outside world continued to trickle into Japan via Dutch traders. A thriving school of "Dutch learning" sprang up in an attempt to study European advances, and there was even a limited knowledge of a place called "Amerika"—described in one book as a fanciful land where people ate human flesh and worshiped the devil.[2] Some Japanese scholars eventually possessed information on America accurate enough to surprise the first Americans who went to Japan in 1853, but it is safe to say that the average Japanese person had never heard of such a distant place.

In the North American colonies people knew as little about Japan as the Japanese knew about them. There was irony in this, however, because had it not been for Japan most of the European immigrants probably would never have made it to the New World in the first place. In the thirteenth century Marco Polo's secondhand reports of an island east of China called "Cipango" had fired the Europeans' imagination. Cipango's residents supposedly ate foreigners if they caught them, but there were thick red pearls, "precious stones," and gold "in great abundance" (slabs of gold two fingers thick were said to line the king's palace).[3] In 1492, when Christopher Columbus sailed across the Atlantic, he was actually searching for a western shortcut to both Cipango and China. Badly underestimating the circumference of the earth, and not realizing that an entire continent blocked his way, when he reached Cuba he was at first convinced that he had landed—not in America—but in Japan.[4]

As with Columbus, whatever the early North American colonists knew about Japan would have continued to come indirectly via Europe, from Portuguese, Spanish, English, and—later—Dutch reports. For anyone interested in such a faraway place, the information available would have continued to be ancient, filtered, fragmentary, and unreliable.

Soon after the United States was born as a nation there was some limited but direct contact between American and Japanese people. In 1791 an American ship visited a Japanese island on the way back from China, but wisely did not try to stay long.[5] Also, between 1797 and 1809 (during the Napoleonic wars) the Dutch were afraid of being attacked by British warships, so they chartered several American ships to fly the Dutch flag and used them in their trade with Japan.[6]

The Japanese isolation policies were nothing to be trifled with. The Portuguese sent one ship to Japan in 1640 to beg that the ban on contact be lifted, only to have the ship burned and most of the crew executed.[7] And in the early nineteenth century, more than one American ship that came too close to Japan's coastline was fired upon or driven off. But not even the most draconian policies could stop the forces of nature. Japan and the American continent, although separated by the Pacific Ocean, are joined by it.

The Castaways

The first Japanese to spend time on United States soil, and the first Americans to spend time in Japan were, in fact, involuntary visitors—castaways. By the early nineteenth century, hundreds of U.S. whaling ships were operating off the coast of Japan. Some found themselves in distress in the area and some had crew members marooned on Japanese soil, arrested, sent to Nagasaki, and deported. Other American ships, cruising the Pacific, began picking up shipwrecked Japanese fishermen.

The most famous Japanese castaway was Manjiro Nakahama. He was rescued by an American whaler in 1841 after being marooned on a tiny Pacific island for six months. A teenager at the time, he was sent to Massachusetts, where he studied English, mathematics, surveying, and navigation, and took the name John Mung. One of the first Japanese to learn English fluently and to have a good knowledge of the United States, in 1851 he boldly returned to Japan, and after intensive interrogation by the authorities was allowed to stay. Curious Japanese officials carefully recorded his comments on American life and his observations of Americans as being, among other things, unusually tall and prone to quaint customs such as making love openly, but also a "sturdy, vigorous, capable, and warm-hearted people." America was, Manjiro insisted, not a land of barbarians but a fine nation in many ways more advanced than Japan. He was never completely trusted by the shogunate, yet after the feudal government collapsed he proved of great service to his country as a teacher and translator.[8] He is a hero in Japan today and the subject of books, plays, and films.

Other Japanese sailors in distress drifted even farther than Manjiro. The "Japan current," or Kuroshio, sweeps by the coast of Japan, across the northern Pacific, and down the west coast of North America. There is a record of a Captain Jukichi whose ship was blown off course and disabled in 1813, who drifted a year and a half and arrived on the California coast, near what is now Santa Barbara, thinking he was landing in Nagasaki. Later, in 1834, three men drifted seventeen months to the Pacific Northwest of America, landing near the Columbia River. After being temporarily enslaved by Indians, they were released to a local Hudson's Bay Company sea captain. These unfortunate souls thereafter were sent to England and then China, and after abortive attempts to return to Japan lived out their lives in Singapore and Macao, one of them marrying an English woman and another reportedly marrying the daughter of American missionaries.[9] Their odyssey made a deep impression on many, and one person whom they particularly affected was the "half-breed" son of a Hudson's Bay official and a Native American Chinook woman in the Oregon area, a man named Ranald MacDonald.

Of no relation to the hamburger chain that would much later invade Japan, MacDonald became the first American to spend time in Japan of his own volition. As he wrote much later in a fascinating autobiography, *Japan: Story of Adventure of Ranald MacDonald, First teacher of English in Japan A.D. 1848–1849,* "Japan was our next neighbor across the way— only the placid sea, the Pacific, between us."[10] Perhaps because he felt a racial affinity with what he heard about the Japanese, he came to believe that Japan was "the land of his ancestors" (an idea remarkably ahead of its time given that Native Americans are now believed to have come from Asia), and he resolved to go there to become an interpreter and someday make his fame and fortune. In 1845 he signed on as a crew member with an American whaling ship out of New York. After many adventures around the world, in 1848 he persuaded the captain to set him adrift in a small boat off the coast of Hokkaido, Japan's most northernmost island. He deliberately capsized his boat near shore to make it look as though he had been shipwrecked, and hoped he would be allowed to stay.

Unfortunately for MacDonald, he was soon discovered by the local Japanese officials and samurai in the area. He was placed under arrest and shipped to the southern port of Nagasaki, where he was imprisoned, interrogated, and forced to step on an image of the Virgin Mary and child to make certain he was not a proselytizing Catholic (as a Protestant, this gave him no particular problem). After ten months of confinement in a room seven feet by nine feet, he was released to an American ship that had approached Nagasaki trying to rescue some other stranded American sailors. The other sailors, apparently quite a rough lot, had received brutal treatment, but MacDonald, perhaps because of his race, his open mind, and positive attitude, had been treated well and made many friends. He had spent much of his time trying to learn Japanese and teaching his captors English. As he wrote later, of all the peoples he had met in his travels, both civilized and uncivilized, "there are none to whom I feel more kindly—more grateful—than my old hosts of Japan; none whom I esteem more highly."[11]

Forced Contacts

The increased contact between Japanese and Americans in the mid-nineteenth century was not just the result of shipwrecks and tides. It was also the result of technology and of the "manifest destiny" of America. Improved ship designs—clipper ships, and later steamships—had vastly speeded up ocean travel. And there wasn't as far to travel. Through giant land purchases and wars, the borders of the United States had been pushed rapidly westward, all the way to the Pacific coast. By 1850, the United States and Japan were neighbors separated by five thousand miles, and it was theoretically possible to sail from San Francisco to Tokyo in only twenty days.

Japan's policy of isolation ended in 1853, when an armed U.S. fleet headed by Commodore Matthew Perry showed up in Tokyo Bay and demanded that it end. U.S.-British rivalry was growing in the Pacific, and Perry and the U.S. government wanted better treatment for American sailors and whaling ships when they were in trouble, coaling stations for steamships crossing the Pacific on the way to China, and, if possible, the opportunity to engage in trade. Perry arrived at a time when this "hermit kingdom" was creaking and groaning from internal contradictions, and he became the catalyst for a virtual revolution.

What happened after Perry's arrival is well known—how the Japanese jettisoned their swords and feudal system of government, imported and embraced Western technology, built up their economy, and within a frenzied fifty years modernized enough to rival European nations in the area; how Japan took the path of militarism in the mid-twentieth century and became embroiled in war with the United States, and how, after the war, it rose, phoenixlike from the ashes, to become one of the world's most powerful economic and technological superstates.

What is often forgotten is the special relationship that Perry's visit established between Japan and the United States. Although the U.S. rudely rousted Japan from its slumbering isolation, in very real ways it also helped Japan modernize and take its first faltering steps onto the world stage, almost acting as a mentor nation in the late nineteenth century. Japan modeled its new educational system after that of Germany and its navy after that of Great Britain, and by no means relied on the United States alone, but because of a shared ocean and physical closeness the United States' influence on Japan was enormous. America provided hundreds of missionaries, teachers, and technical experts to Japan, some of whom—like William S. Clark, who in 1867 founded what is now Hokkaido University and exhorted his eager students with the now-famous admonition, "Boys be ambitious"—are still household words in Japan today. Many of the early Americans to deal with Japan were also genuinely worried how Japan would fare exposed to the modern world and had a real concern for its well-being as a nation. When Townsend Harris, the first U.S. consul, negotiated the Treaty of Amity and Commerce with Japan in 1858, he specifically included a clause that said, "The President of the United States, at the request of the Japanese Government, will act as a friendly mediator in such matters of difference as may arise between the Government of Japan and any European power."[12]

Japan was fortunate its isolation was ended by the United States. In the mid-nineteenth century the European colonial powers were in one of their most expansionist and rapacious phases, and a type of "social Darwinism," or a belief in the survival of the fittest of nations, had broader acceptance than Darwin's theory of evolution itself would find. Much of Asia, including China, was already being ruthlessly carved up by the rapidly expanding Europeans. Though the United States was itself not free from imperialistic leanings, it was at a phase of its history where it was still trying to digest the huge new territories it had acquired in the West. And it was still a young nation, where the ideology that had led to independence from England in the first place—a belief in the evils of colonialism—had not yet completely faded.

Had not the Americans arrived in Japan to demand change when they did, it is highly likely that other, less friendly powers would have, and Japan's transition to a modern nation might have been far more difficult. Technologically backward Japan might even have been gobbled up entirely. As would happen much later again after World War II, when the U.S. prevented the partitioning of Japan like Germany and Korea, America probably helped preserve Japan's territorial integrity.

Closer and Closer

Today Japan and the United States are much closer neighbors than they were in 1853, when they were separated by over 5,000 miles. The capital of our fiftieth state, Honolulu, is only 3,859 miles from Tokyo. Guam, "Where American's Day Begins," is only 800 miles from Tokyo if one measures from the island of Iwo Jima, which through a jurisdictional quirk is technically part of distant, metropolitan Tokyo. And as the physical distance between our two nations has shrunk, the means to cover it has vastly improved. Instead of treacherous ocean voyages of months, we are separated by plane rides of mere hours. With a good tailwind today, it takes only eight and a half hours to fly from Tokyo to San Francisco, or about the same time it takes to drive between Los Angeles and San Francisco.

A sense of proximity between nations is of course not determined merely by physical miles. In today's world it is also determined by the ease and cost of communications, cultural similarities, the state of political relations, and even currency exchange rates. In the first case, fiber optic cables, satellite transmissions, phones, modems, and facsimile machines have brought Japan closer than anyone could have dreamed even fifty years ago. Phone calls to Tokyo are now sometimes clearer than those made around the block. Fax messages are instantaneous, and cost less to Japan than to neighboring Mexico. And the amount of communication between the two nations is exploding. According to FCC surveys, calls from the United States to Japan increased fourteen fold between 1980 and 1990, and now are exceeded only by those to the United Kingdom and Germany.[13] A time difference of up to twenty hours still exists between Japan and America, but even this can be used to advantage. If a company in Tokyo urgently needs a document translated into English overnight, rather than hiring someone locally it can use a translator in America equipped with a fax and a modem; the American works at his or her regular daytime schedule, for lower rates, and the finished product arrives in Tokyo in the morning.

Today Japan and America are like two humans with interconnected circulatory and nervous systems. But instead of veins and arteries, we have ships and airplanes carrying people and goods. Instead of nerves and synapses, we have phones, faxes, and satellites, zapping increasingly digitalized information back and forth around the clock, in the form of letters, voices, pictures, and money. We not only communicate; we are literally wired together.

The Trade Connection

The most visible link between Japan and the United States today is trade in physical goods and services. Trade in goods is the easiest component of our relationship for most people to understand because we live with, touch, and enjoy each other's products everyday. In the U.S. we park Japanese cars in our garages, and decorate our living rooms, kitchens, and bedrooms with artfully designed Japanese electronic gizmos. We wear Japanese Walkmans on our heads when we go for walks, and we increasingly wear Japanese condoms when we have sex. But we are not alone in this intimacy with another nation's products. Despite all the talk about how "closed" the Japanese market is, trade is by no means a one-way street. Japanese gulp down Coca-Cola, puff Marlboros, shave with Schick razors, use Kodak film, and listen to hip-hop CDs. They buy Sunkist oranges and California wine, and annually eat approximately 12,000 tons of U.S. hamburger beef at over 820 "Macs," as McDonald's fast food restaurants are affectionately called.[14] It is thus not surprising that many young Americans think Honda is an American car company or that Pac Man and Super Mario are American characters, while many young Japanese think McDonald's is a Japanese institution.

The visible part of the trade in goods and services is only the tip of a gigantic iceberg. When Japanese eat tofu, they rarely think about the fact that it is made almost entirely from soybeans grown in the United States. When they use Japan's best-selling NEC personal computers, they rarely think about the fact that the operating system and the central processing unit—the brains of the computer—usually come from America. Likewise, when Americans use an Apple computer, how many of us are aware that almost all the components inside it, save for the motherboard, come from Japan? Or, when we ride in our Ford Taurus SHO sedans, that the engines are made by Yamaha in Japan?

Japan is currently the second largest market for U.S. goods, next to Canada, and the United States is by far and away the largest customer for Japan's exports. But in addition to trading with each other, Japan and America also own large parts of each other. In 1993, Japan was the second largest investor in the U.S. economy, and the U.S. was by far the largest direct foreign investor in Japan. American auto companies complain loudly about their Japanese competitors, yet rarely mention how much of those competitors they own. At one point in the 1980s Chrysler owned 24 percent of Mitsubishi.[15] In 1993, General Motors owned 3.5 percent of Suzuki and 37.5 percent of Isuzu, while Ford owned 24.5 percent of Mazda. The vice president of Isuzu Motors and a director of Mazda Motor Corp were both U.S. citizens.[16]

Foreign trade enables us to obtain or enjoy things that for one reason or another we do not make or produce ourselves (such as Walkmans and

CD players in the case of America, or jumbo jets in the case of Japan). Japanese investment in the U.S. enables us to raise capital, or money. Japanese money earned from selling us VCRs and automobiles is plowed back into the American stock market and U.S. government treasuries, into new factories being built in America under Japanese ownership, and into American land and buildings. This money helps prop up our debt-ridden government and provides hundreds of thousands of us with jobs.

The more trade and investment flourishes, the more it binds our societies together and makes us truly interdependent. Ever since World War II, Japan has been so dependent on the United States that Japanese have long joked that "when America sneezes, Japan catches a cold." Today, because of heavy two-way trade and complex cross-investing, the situation is much more of a two-way street. Corporate alliances between Japan and America, if charted, would look like a tangled mass of spaghetti. Should America's exports of food to Japan suddenly halt, Japan would starve to death. Should all Japanese components used in American machinery suddenly vaporize, America's high-tech civilization would come to a screeching halt. In 1992, when the Japanese stock market went into a tailspin, Wall Street got the jitters. As author Peter Hadfield warned in his book *Sixty Seconds That Will Change the World: The Coming Tokyo Earthquake*, our economies are so intertwined that a major earthquake in Japan's capital city might very well wreak havoc with the U.S. economy.[17] For all the irritations and arguments over trade imbalances and who is being "fair" or "unfair," mutual trade and investment have linked our fates and made the idea of outright war, if not unthinkable, at least extraordinarily painful to contemplate.

The Human Bond

The most important link between Japan and America today is not money or things but people, for as people shuttle back and forth they form bonds and friendships. According to Japanese government statistics, in

1991 North America was the most popular destination for Japanese travelers outside of Asia, with over 3.5 million visitors. Similarly, it was also where the most Japanese nationals—over a quarter of a million—were living abroad. Conversely, more U.S. citizens (over half a million) visited Japan in 1991 and more U.S. civilians were registered residents of Japan than any other nationality except for Filipinos, Koreans, and Chinese (the last two being the traditional minority groups in Japan, many of whom have lived in Japan for generations but have been discouraged from obtaining citizenship).[18]

Americans go to Japan for business, pleasure, and study, but they are also sent there as members of the U.S. military. Since 1951 the Japan-United States security treaty has been the linchpin in the U.S.-Japan relationship. The bonds these mostly male, mostly ordinary Americans have formed while serving in Japan in the military have been its human glue. In July 1993 there were 48,612 U.S. military personnel stationed at U.S. bases throughout Japan, and 12,601 members of the U.S. Seventh Fleet afloat whose families lived on shore; altogether there were also 46,776 military dependents in Japan. Yet the number of Americans who have been in Japan because of the military connection is far greater than this. If one counted every American who has passed through Japan as a GI during the Occupation, the Korean War, the Vietnam War, or subsequently, the total would easily exceed ten million.[19]

No mention of an interchange of people can be complete without a mention of the role of immigration. It has made the relationship between Japan and the United States unlike the relationship Japan has with any other nation, except perhaps Brazil.

For the obvious reasons of population pressures and ideology, except for a few Americans who marry Japanese or become professional sumo wrestlers almost all of the immigration has been from Japan to the United States, which has historically welcomed and depended on immigrants. The first true immigrant from Japan was Hikozo Hamada, a young castaway in the Pacific who was saved by an American sailing ship in 1850 and taken to the United States. Eventually baptized and given the Christian name "Joseph Heco," he became a naturalized U.S. citizen and served his new country well as an interpreter and civil servant in its new relations with Japan. Favored by many in high positions, he met with Presidents Buchanan and Lincoln.

After Japan opened itself to the world, Heco was quickly joined by other Japanese, who flocked to the New World in exactly the same spirit as the Irish, Germans, Norwegians, English, and others, trying to escape poverty, oppression, and overpopulation and hoping for a better life. Japanese immigration to the U.S. peaked in 1906, and today's Japanese-Americans (who are mostly third-and-fourth generation descendants of the earlier immigrants) number only around 847,000, or 0.3 percent of the total U.S. population.[20] But their contribution to society far outweighs their number. Often patronizingly referred to in the media as the "model minority," they rank higher in educational and income level than nearly every other ethnic group, including European-Americans. Once farmers, gardeners, and restaurant operators and heavily discriminated against, they are now dentists, lawyers, and respected artists, architects, and politicians.

Whether first or fifth generation, today's Japanese-Americans have their feet and their souls planted firmly on American soil. They have no more connection to Japan than German-Americans have to Germany, although for racial reasons (as during World War II, when they were incarcerated in concentration camps), they tend to bear the brunt of anti-Japanese prejudice whenever tensions flare between the U.S. and Japan. They are merely another hyphenated ingredient in the still-simmering multicultural goulash of modern American society.

It is interesting to note—now that Japan's citizens are among the world's most prosperous and the Japanese media reflect the same negative images of the United States as Americans see on their own televisions—that immigration from Japan is still taking place, albeit at a much reduced level. In 1991 and 1992, the Japanese media marveled that after Irish and Polish, Japanese comprised the third largest group of applicants for Green

Cards, or permanent resident permits, that were being given away in a lottery in the United States.[21]

Like that of other ethnic groups, the contribution of immigrants from Japan is not just cultural. Japanese-Americans have one of the highest rates of marrying outside their racial group of any "minority." Furthermore, even though during the Occupation of Japan from 1945 to 1952 there were still many U.S. legal and social barriers to interracial marriage, American GIs still fell in love with, married, and brought back between ten and fifty thousand Japanese women as so-called "war brides" (and left behind over ten thousand mixed-blood children).[22] More and more Americans who do not consider themselves ethnically Japanese, and more and more Japanese who do not consider themselves ethnically American, are therefore directly connected to each other by marriage and by blood.

Mind Meld East

If Japan and America have grown closer in virtual distance, Japanese and American people have also grown together in the culture of the mind. It has long been popular to write books about how "different" Japanese are from Americans; the libraries in both nations are full of them. While there are indeed profound and often frustrating differences between our two societies, it is important to realize how similar we have become; how we increasingly share the same interests and values, how we increasingly *think* alike. If we concentrate so much on differences we forget how vast the distance between American and Japanese cultures used to be, and we overlook how much Japanese culture is influencing us, just as we are influencing it.

Clearly, Japan has moved far more in our direction than we have in its direction. Shortly after Perry arrived in Japan, Japan sent its first official mission to the United States. One of the members of this group was a young man named Yukichi Fukuzawa, and he was so impressed with what he saw in America that he later became one of the main proponents of modernization. In 1885, in his enormously influential essay "Datsu-a-ron" [A Theory for Abandoning Asia], Fukuzawa advocated that Japan distance itself from technologically backward Asia and emulate the United States and Europe.[23]

Since then, Japan has altered so many core aspects of its society that in the 1980s it became common for the media in both America and Japan to refer to Japan as being part of the group of "Western" nations. Today's Japanese have changed the way they tell time and record dates, and they have adopted international or U.S. standards in everything from clothing to construction to telecommunications. In the postwar period especially, the United States has been overwhelmingly the model of choice.

A Japanese young man today on his day off is very likely to wear Converse sneakers, Levi's jeans, and a T-shirt, be a fanatic fan of a Japanese baseball team (which usually includes a couple of professional American players), and if wealthy enough, live in a prefabricated house made with U.S.-style two-by-four lumber. A young Japanese woman may eat Oreos for a snack, watch CNN news with simultaneous interpretation and sumo wrestling matches with American-born champions, read Canadian Harlequin Romances or *Newsweek* in translation, dance at a disco to American rap music, and wear a baseball cap turned fashionably backward. Both man and woman probably hum melodies that are major in scale (instead of the traditional Japanese minor, pentatonic scale), and tap their feet to an American rock beat. Both probably also celebrate Father's Day and Mother's Day, and—while not Christians—observe commercialized variants of Christmas, Halloween, and Valentine's Day.

Does Anybody Here Speak English?

When Americans and Japanese first came into contact with each other only a hundred and fifty years ago, they had almost nothing in common except their basic humanity. They existed in separate realities. They were not only of different races, but they wore entirely different clothes, had weirdly different hairstyles, ate completely different food, worshiped different gods, maintained different philosophies of government, different calendars, and different time systems, and spoke utterly unrelated languages with different systems of logic. When Commodore Perry first negotiated with the Japanese in 1853 and 1854, it is amazing that he was able to communicate anything at all.

Despite the fact that the brave young American adventurer, Ranald MacDonald, had taught some English to the Japanese interpreters in Nagasaki before Perry arrived, the official languages of the negotiators were neither English nor Japanese, but Dutch and Chinese. When Perry said one thing in English, an American interpreter would struggle to render it into Dutch and then relay this to his Japanese interpreter counterpart, who (mostly familiar with an archaic form of Dutch) would then struggle to translate the Dutch into Japanese for his superiors. But even if both sides had had interpreters who could speak Japanese and English they still would have run into problems. Today, with all our shared knowledge, our experience in communicating, and our skilled "simultaneous interpreters" with headphones sitting in special booths, the room for serious mistakes when Japanese and Americans communicate is still enormous, and they occur with depressing regularity. Japanese is not a particularly difficult language, but its structure and cultural context are very different from those of English. Japanese uses four different writing systems (Chinese ideograms, two phonetic scripts, and the roman alphabet), and it has elevated being ambiguous to the level of an art form—so much so that serious misunderstandings often ensue even among Japanese people themselves.

Today's Japanese are notorious for their poor English ability, but this is not for their lack of trying. They make enormous efforts to learn English. Those who graduate from college typically have studied English for ten years. After college, they may continue to study at one of almost ten thousand private schools usually staffed with American or British teachers. Japan has one of the world's largest markets for foreign-language learning, and it has become so popular to learn English—particularly "American English"—that, as any foreigner teaching there will attest, many people study not just to learn English but simply to enhance their social status.

Even before they begin studying English, however, Japanese people know many English words that have been absorbed into their language. A few years back a popular writer named Yoshinori Shimizu wrote a short story titled "Jobun," or "Introduction," in which he used pseudo "comparative linguistics" to "prove" that the English language was extremely indebted to Japanese. The English word "name," he claimed, really comes from the Japanese *namae* (name); "kill" comes from the Japanese *kiru* (to cut, slash, or kill with a sword), and so on.[24] It was all a very obvious parody, of course. As nearly all Japanese know, their language has adopted so many English words in the last one hundred and fifty years that a samurai transported to the present day from the early eighteenth century would be completely befuddled.

Unlike the French, Japanese people rarely make a deliberate effort to come up with native equivalents for English terms, and instead embrace them as is. The English words may be pronounced differently (as in *raifu-waaku*, for "life's work"), truncated or abbreviated (as in *nega*, for "negative," or *FA*, for "factory automation"), telescoped (as in *pasokon*, for "personal computer," or *sekuhara*, for "sexual harassment"), or, in what is called *wasei-eigo*, or "Japanese-manufactured English," entirely made up (an example being *pushuhon*, or "push phone," for "touch-tone telephones" or *bodikon gyaru*, "body conscious gal," for young women who pay a great deal of attention to their physical looks). The words nonetheless remain identifiably English. Unlike the writing systems of most languages, such as English, Spanish, or even Korean, which quickly digest foreign words, in the Japanese language English words also remain *visually* identifiable, for they are written in an angular script—*katakana*—reserved mainly for foreign words.

In daily life, rice on a plate is *raisu,* beds are *beddo,* toilets are *toire,* sex is *sekkusu,* and on and on. In the computer *(konpyuuta)* industry, where the latest terminology still comes from the United States *(Amerika),* manuals *(manyuaru)* are so littered with words like *furoppii disku* (floppy disk), *doraibu* (drive), *modemu* (modem), *purintaa* (printer), and *kiiboodo* (keyboard), one sometimes wonders why they don't just write the whole thing in English. On rock music programs on the radio or television, a *diijei* (DJ) may announce a song with adjectives like *fankii,* (funky), *rajikaru* (radical), and *hebii saundo* (heavy sound), and layer his or her entire patter with heavy "American" accents. Sometimes it seems that the only thing Japanese about DJ speech is the grammar and connecting particles.

It is not just English nouns and adjectives that are adopted in Japan. Prepositions are used, too. A public message poster in 1993 promoted sincerity and good behavior with the touchingly sweet *haato in, manaa appu* (heart in, manners up). In the last ten years it has also been fashionable to use the English particle "the" *(za)* in book titles. Rural Tottori Prefecture, in an extensive campaign to spiff up its image, uses the convoluted-in-English but somehow-catchy-in-Japanese slogan *Imeeji za Tottori* (Image the Tottori).

Film distributors now translate fewer and fewer movie titles into Japanese and simply render them in *katakana. Dances with Wolves* in Japan was thus publicized as the confusing tongue twister—*dansu uizu urubuzu.* In the advertising world, English is often used because it is believed to have a special "cachet." In the 1980s, when many of Japan's semigovernmental organizations were privatized, the new companies even stopped writing their names in Japanese and began using English initials—the telephone monopoly, Nihon Denshin Denwa Kosha (or Denden Kosha) thus became NTT, and the national railways, Nihon Kokuyu Tetsudo (or Kokutetsu), became JR. One can appreciate the true implications of this by imagining General Motors or IBM deciding to write its name in the United States with Japanese *kanji* characters.

Some unaltered English is used gratuitously and for visual effect on posters, shopping bags, and clothes. The quality of this English has improved over the last few decades, but still the meanings are often opaque and the words seem randomly selected. Many foreigners collect the best examples. Everyone who has lived in Japan for a long time still has a tale or two about some innocent-looking rural grandmother wearing a T-shirt printed with fractured English proclaiming that she wants to fornicate with young maidens. As one foreign writer noted from the advertising copy on a notebook, the Japanese are "FANS OF ANYTHING AND EVERYTHING ENGLISHED."[25]

The Americanization of the Japanese Mind

English has had a profound effect not only on the way Japanese speak their language, but on how they perceive reality.

First, as a result of translating and applying information from the "West," the surface appearance of modern Japanese urban civilization—the technology, the machines, the buildings—is now the same as America's. Even if we do not speak each other's language, we inhabit similar physical worlds and share the common language of modern science and technology; we increasingly talk and think about the same things, in the same way.

Second, not just technical information, but movies, TV shows, song lyrics, pure literature, pop literature, and trash are translated into Japanese today at a mind-boggling volume and speed (many American books are now published in Japanese at almost the same time they appear in English). Since not all this translation work is done particularly well, many Japanese have ironically developed a unique tolerance for their own language as rendered in a sort of "translation-ese." As early as 1931, in his paper "Foreign Influences in the Japanese Language," Professor Sanki Ichikawa of Tokyo Imperial University noted that while many other cultures borrowed foreign words, in Japan the borrowing of English was so heavy that it was even affecting the fundamental structure of the language, increasing use of the passive voice, the progressive tense, and the causative as well as of personal pronouns.[26] Colloquialisms originally alien to the Japanese language—awkward expressions like *kusa no ne undo* (grassroots movement) and *yoru ga wakai* (the "night is young," instead of the original Japanese concept of "the night is still long")—have become accepted in the modern vocabulary. When working as an interpreter today for younger generations of Japanese and Americans of similar socioeconomic backgrounds, it is hard not to be amazed at how similar our sense of humor, our speech rhythms, and even our thought patterns have become. Inscrutable Eastern ways of thinking are increasingly becoming just like inscrutable Western ways of thinking.

This English-ization and Americanization of the Japanese mind is taking place at the highest and most hidebound levels of society. The current emperor of Japan was tutored as a young man by American Quaker Elizabeth Gray Vining; his son, the crown prince, a graduate of Oxford University in England, is married to the enormously popular Masako Owada, a former commoner. Masako—the future empress of Japan—is not only a Harvard graduate who speaks perfect English, but, like an increasing number of offspring of Japanese international businessmen, the product of an American public high school.

Finally, Japanese people have not only begun to think like Americans—they have begun to look more like them. This is meant literally, and not just in the sense that they wear the same type of clothes, affect American fashions, or sometimes try to create a more "Western" look by dyeing, curling, or kinking their hair, by wearing colored contact lenses, and by having operations to achieve a "rounder" eye. Among younger generations, because of better, protein-rich diets (more hamburgers) and different life styles (less kneeling and more use of chairs), once bowed and short legs have straightened, and body proportions and even facial shapes have changed accordingly. Americans who still think of Japanese as "short, little people" are going to be in for a very rude shock in the next few years. The height of the average Japanese male has increased four inches in the last three decades. According to one Ministry of Education survey, the average thirteen-year-old boy in 1990 was an astounding seven inches taller than his counterpart in 1950.[27]

Mind Meld West

As Japan has become more like America, so has America become more like Japan. Japan's influence on America is subtle, but it is not new. The men who made up Japan's first official embassy to the United States in 1860 were received like conquering heroes, with parades and continuous festivities (included in the group were Manjiro, acting as an interpreter, and Yukichi Fukuzawa). Because of Japan's long isolation, many aspects of its culture seemed simultaneously archaic, novel, and strange to the Americans. They were fascinated by the samurais' odd dress, their swords, and their shaved heads. A mania for things Japanese soon developed. But the mania was not just for things. Japanese art helped set off the movement called "Japonisme" in both Europe and the United States that helped artists free themselves from literal representations and experiment with impressionist and abstract depictions of reality. And even more than art, Americans soon found themselves influenced by Japanese poetry and literature.

As Sanehide Kodama writes in his book *American Poetry and Japanese Culture*, "There may be no country in the world outside of Japan in which the traditional Japanese values have been more appreciated by its artists than the United States."[28]

In 1860, Walt Whitman saw a parade by the first Japanese mission in New York and got so inspired that he wrote a poem titled "The Errand Bearers." Published in the *New York Times*, the poem portrayed a symbolic meeting of East and West and the possibilities for human brotherhood. Whitman believed, according to Kodama, that the Japanese were messengers of the great Eastern philosophies and that they would "make Americans realize the necessity of facing space, the 'kosmos,' which would enable them to see the transcendental nature of man in the vast and har-moniously ordered system of the universe."[29]

The Arts

Ever since Whitman, American poets and writers have been using Japan as a well into which they can dip for intellectual inspiration. At times this has resulted in a puerile quest for the exotic, or an uncritical belief that everything Japanese is superior and "exquisite." But when used with care, the Japanese well has enabled artists to establish a new frame of reference and a new perspective on reality.

The list of writers and artists who have fallen in love with Japan is long. One of them, Lafcadio Hearn (born in Greece and technically a British citizen but herein claimed as an American), had a life-long fasci-nation with the exotic. When he went to Japan in 1890 he found so much to satisfy his interests that he married a Japanese woman, took a Japanese name (Koizumi Yakumo), and became a naturalized Japanese citizen. Un-fortunately, Hearn liked the old Japan even more than the Japanese did, and he became distressed at the rate of Japan's modernization and the destruction of its traditional culture.

Other writers and poets, rather than writing about Japan, attempted to incorporate Japanese poetic devices into the English language. Amy Lowell, Ezra Pound, Carl Sandburg, T.S. Eliot, and Richard Wright were all deeply influenced by Japanese poetry, and by haiku in particular. Haiku, the best known form of Japanese poetry, mixes specific seasonal images in a simple but rigid structure of three lines of five, seven, and five sylla-bles. The best haiku encapsulate a powerful experience in a few words. To American poets raised in the Western tradition of rhyming and meter, haiku were both a revelation and a revolutionary force. As Earl Miner comments in *The Japanese Tradition in British and American Literature*, "before Japanese poetry became known to the west, few poets would have felt they dared to write a short poem about a moth and the moon unless they could discover a suitable moral to draw from the description."[30] Japanese theater, especially Kabuki and Noh, was also an eye-opener for American writers. Kabuki consists of highly theatrical and colorful plays originally developed for commoners in Japan, while Noh contains highly stylized, classical performances traditionally enjoyed by the nobility. Ezra Pound, often said to be one of the greatest poets of the twentieth century (and regarded as something of a nut for his political views), was not only a fanatic fan of haiku; he once seriously proposed that the United States give Japan the island of Guam in exchange for two Japanese Noh films.[31]

Mastering Zen

Once Americans began delving deeper into Japanese art and literature they encountered an entirely different aesthetic and worldview. To understand it they also had to learn something about the philosophical underpinnings of Japanese culture and society. And this invariably led to religion and to Zen Buddhism.

Modern Japan is a veritable bazaar of religions and religious sects, with Buddhism and Shinto (the native animist faith) being the two largest and most influential. Although Buddhism originated in India, Zen is a particularly Japanese variant of it. It came to Japan via China, and it emphasized the attainment of a sudden enlightenment, or *satori*, through meditation and the freeing of own's mind from the phenomenal world and from preconceived notions of reality. Like haiku, which it heavily influenced, Zen looked for truth in simplicity and encouraged a streamlined esthetic. Many other Japanese sects and religions have influenced Americans and even gained adherents, but none has had as powerful an impact on the American mind as Zen. Zen concepts have permeated the core of American intellectual culture and become part of our spiritual landscape, so that the influence of Zen on America far exceeds the number of its actual American adherents.

American bookstores usually contain popular works on Zen. Most

Americans, if not familiar with actual Zen teachings, have at least heard of Zen or read a book or two with a title like *Zen and the Art of . . .* (insert *motorcycle maintenance, photography, creative management, writing, hunting,* etc.), and they probably use the word "Zen-like" in conversation as a way of describing something simultaneously profound and puzzling. Many know a Zen *koan* (riddle) or two—like "What is the sound of one hand clapping?"—and tens of thousands of Americans have actually tried Zen meditation.

The Beat generation and writers like Jack Kerouac, Kenneth Rexroth, Allen Ginsberg, Philip Whalen, and Gary Snyder were so affected by Zen that the first wave of Zen in America in the 1950s is often called "Beat Zen." Whalen later became a Zen priest in San Francisco. Rexroth and Snyder both learned to read Japanese and translated many haiku and other Japanese poems. Snyder (the Japan-bound Japhy Ryder character in Jack Kerouac's *The Dharma Bums*) lived for a time in a Kyoto monastery and later married a Japanese woman; he went on to blend Buddhist concepts with Native American beliefs and to help create the philosophical underpinnings of the present-day ecology movement.

But it is not only poets who have been influenced by Zen. One could easily construct an elaborate flow chart showing how Zen Buddhist ideas have been transmitted directly and indirectly into the heart of American culture, profoundly influencing politicians such as Jerry Brown, musicians such as John Cage, and even the Grateful Dead and the entire hippy generation.

What is it that so attracts Americans about Zen? One answer comes from the six-foot-five-inch-tall son of American Christian missionaries who now goes by the name Daigaku, meaning "Great Mountain." Daigaku has been meditating as a Zen monk over seventeen years in a temple in rural Japan. "In mainstream Judeo-Christianity," he says, "most people have a dualistic view of God and Man. In Buddhism everything is Buddha. It's just a matter of waking up to that, and *zazen,* or meditating, is the means to do it. Buddhism is the only religion that has the guts to really deal with the three most difficult aspects of the ego; greed, anger, and ignorance. Zen is the way of liberation from the ego-self."[32]

Sushi and Comic Books

Naturally, most influences from Japan roll into the United States on a far less spiritual plane than haiku and Zen. We are, in fact, currently experiencing a cultural cross-pollination of colossal, mass-market proportions.

Just as the United States exported baseball to Japan (where it is arguably more popular than in its birthplace), Japan has exported several of its "sports" to the United States. Japanese martial arts such as karate, judo, and aikido, with their emphasis on spiritual as well as physical discipline, have found fertile soil in the United States; towns of even modest size today have at least one karate school, filled with people learning self-defense or acting out samurai-ninja fantasies. Just as American educators once helped Japanese modernize their school systems, now most American cities have places that teach math and other subjects with the Kumon method of learning or teach violin with the Suzuki method.

And just as American food, especially fast food, has permeated the Japanese diet, so has Japanese food increasingly become part of our own culinary landscape. Japanese instant noodles and tofu are available everywhere; the latter, in an interesting example of American innovation, is winning fans in low-fat frozen yogurt imitations and in "tofu" burgers and shakes. Japanese restaurants have been around as long as Japanese immigrants, but in the last ten years they have exploded in popularity. Most Americans would have been nauseated by the thought of eating raw fish even fifteen years ago, but on the coasts today sushi is high fashion. It is no longer unusual to see Americans at sushi bars who can order their favorite raw fish *only* by their Japanese names, who know sea urchin as *uni*, spanish mackerel as *aji*, and yellow tail as *hamachi*.

The real barometer of how much Japanese culture America is absorbing can be found in a place one would least expect it—American pop culture. Pop culture is sometimes regarded as an almost exclusive province of America—our last bastion of unrivaled competitiveness and our most successful export. But young Americans, like their counterparts across the oceans, have their antennas up and pointed toward whatever is interesting, no matter where it originates. And they are increasingly tuned to what is happening in Japan.

Japanese popular music is starting to seep into the United States in such diverse genres as jazz, techno-pop, New Age, salsa, and kitsch rock à la the all-girl band Shonen Knife. But the real success story is Japanese animation and comic books. American and Japanese live-action movies have long been influencing each other (witness the transformation of Akira Kurosawa's *Seven Samurai* into John Sturges's *Magnificent Seven*, a 1960 cowboy adventure starring Yul Brynner and Steve McQueen), but in the last ten years Japanese animation and comics have stormed into young America's consciousness. Ironically, both art forms originated in the United States, but in Japan animation (called *anime*) and comic books (*manga*) have developed relatively free from stereotyping and censorship, and have thus flourished in a way they were never able to in the less-permissive United States. Comics in Japan far surpass books in popularity, and comprise nearly 40 percent of all published magazines and books.[33] Animation increasingly rivals live-action films both in box office receipts and TV ratings.

In the U.S., most major comic book publishers now issue translated versions of Japanese manga, but many fans don't even wait for the translations. If they are not literate in Japanese, they scan and "read" the originals, deducing meaning from the pictures. As for animation, a generation of Americans was raised in the 1960s on TV series such as *Astro Boy* and *Speed Racer*. These imports from Japan were so cleverly dubbed that most viewers never even knew they were watching something foreign. Programming content rules have subsequently kept most Japanese shows off the U.S. networks because they are designed for a higher age group (and therefore have a higher erotic and violence quotient than most American children's shows), but full-length animated films are beginning to appear in theaters. In addition, there are now four companies in the United States that specialize in dubbing or subtitling Japanese material for fans. What they do not cover, fans with language skills and access to the right equipment subtitle on their own, circulating pirate video copies among clubs and friends. There are now as many as one hundred "fanzines" published in the United States by local anime and manga clubs scattered across the nation. And there are growing communities of fans that exchange information on computer bulletin boards and national networks such as CompuServe, Genie, and the Internet. Interestingly, many American fans are adults working in the computer and high-tech industries. Since 1991 there have been enough of them to support annual national conventions with attendance in the thousands.

Japanese manga and anime are also helping to inspire American comic artists. The acclaimed artist Frank Miller (who has drawn for the *Batman* and the *Ronin* series, among others) has publicly noted his debt to Japanese manga, in particular to the cinematic layouts and progressions developed in Japan; the best manga, he claims, achieve a "perfect visual storytelling."[34] At least one artist, Ben Dunn, the author of *Ninja High School*, draws original material in a deliberately "Japanese" style expressly for American fans of manga. One of the hallmarks of manga is big, rounded eyes (actually a legacy of the influence of Walt Disney). In a recent interview in *Comics Journal*, Pulitzer Prize–winning comic artist Art Spiegelman, the author of *Maus*, went so far as to claim that American artists in general are now drawing the eyes of their characters bigger again—because of the Japanese influence.[35]

Ultimately, the indirect impact of Japanese manga and anime on American life is far greater than its direct impact. Manga and anime are, for example, also the creative source of the transforming robot toy fad of the eighties, and of hundreds, if not thousands, of the video games which so captivate American children today.

Does Anybody Here Speak Japanese?

Those fascinated by Japanese pop culture obviously have a personal interest in learning the Japanese language, but they are not the only ones studying it today. While the number of Americans learning Japanese still pales in comparison to the number of Japanese learning English, there has nonetheless been an explosion in the popularity of Japanese language courses in American universities and private institutions. People study Japanese out of curiosity, to get a job in international business, to communicate with friends overseas, and—since over half a million Americans now work for Japanese corporations—to communicate better with their new Japanese bosses. Nationally, the number of college students studying Japanese in the U.S. quadrupled between 1980 and 1990, from 11,500 to 45,700.[36]

And sure enough, English is also absorbing more and more Japanese words. English is itself a hybrid of several European languages, and nearly as syncretic and flexible as Japanese. Over the years English has absorbed many Japanese terms, starting with words like "bonze" (priest) from the sixteenth century, "shogun" from the seventeenth century, and "tycoon," "typhoon," "geisha," "rickshaw," and so on from the nineteenth century. Other words, like "kamikaze," "sukiyaki," and "honcho" (which comes from *hancho*, or "group leader"), entered our vocabulary during and after World War II and the Occupation. More recently, a Levi's ad in the 1980s for a slightly fuller cut of trousers used the word "skosh," from the Japanese word *sukoshi*, or "a little," which certainly came in from American GIs. The name of the popular video game in the 1980s, Pac Man, comes from the Japanese word *paku paku*, or "munch munch."

Like the Japanese, when we are exposed to aspects of a different culture for which we have no equivalent vocabulary in our own language, we simply adopt the original foreign words to describe them. More and more Americans begin sleeping on low mats like the Japanese (at the same time more and more Japanese are sleeping on beds like us), and we find Yellow

Pages directories that list the mats under the Japanese word *futon*. A Japanese plant accidentally brought to the U.S. finds itself with no natural enemies and goes berserk in the Southeast, and we refer to the infamous "kudzu." More and more Americans start singing off-key in public with microphones, and we use "karaoke" (meaning "empty orchestra") boxes to provide the musical accompaniment.

Many of the Japanese words that have recently entered the English language reflect Japan's increased influence in technology and industry. Americans whose firms are struggling to incorporate Japanese-style "management techniques" or "quality control" know and use words like *kaizen* (continuous improvement), *keiretsu* (industrial groupings), and even *poka-yoke* (a type of foolproofing). One interesting tendency is for Japanese industry to coin an English word or usage that is then adopted back into English spoken by Americans. This is what happened with the Japanese-invented "mechatronics," which combines "mechanics" and "electronics." The English word "software" was in common use in America, but it was the Japanese who first widely used it to describe movies, records, or any other information-based medium that runs on top of hardware.

Will the English language ever become as saturated with Japanese words as the Japanese language is with English? It is hardly likely, but more than one American has envisioned some sort of hybridization in the future. Poet Ezra Pound was in favor of an international language he called "Japerican" that combined Japanese (because he believed ideograms were necessary to express certain thoughts), English (because it is already so widely spoken), and Italian (because of its simplicity and ease of spelling).[37] In Ridley Scott's 1982 film *Blade Runner*, the writers conjured up a vision of twenty-first century Los Angeles where the masses speak a mixture of English, Spanish, and Japanese. And one of the hallmarks of the contemporary cyberpunk genre of American science fiction, whether novels like William Gibson's *Neuromancer* or TV shows like Oliver Stone's "Wild Palms," is a heavy dose of "Japanese" settings, imagery, and terminology.

Consumer Culture

Language, investment, food, and so on are only the most obvious aspects of how Japanese culture influences us today. The most significant influences may be more subtle, affecting our social behavior, our lifestyles, and even our sense of beauty. American inventions and technology—the radio, the television, and the computer—have changed the way people around the world work, communicate, and spend their leisure time. Similarly, Japanese products, even if their underlying technology was invented in America, reflect Japanese culture in the way they are designed and made and used. The hallmarks of Japanese consumer goods—light weight, miniaturization, high quality relative to cost, and an overwhelming commercial orientation—are at least partially driven by Japanese space requirements, esthetics, traditions of craftsmanship, and a need to export. The Walkman style of tape recorder, for example, emerged from an overcrowded, technological society that prizes miniaturization and the ability to do things without bothering others. The Japanese video games to which American children are addicted have a Japanese cultural component to them, too, in characters and plot and (like Walkmans) in the somewhat autistic lifestyle they promote. Facsimile machines, while first developed in the United States, were first made affordable and practical in Japan, where telexes and typewriters were too awkward to use as a means of transmitting handwritten messages quickly.

Ultimately, Japanese products and their technology can have a profound influence on the way we view Japan itself. After meeting with President Clinton in 1993, then prime minister Kiichi Miyazawa commented, "It was the first time the U.S. and Japan were able to interact as adults. During World War II former President Bush was shot down [by Japan] and nearly drowned near Iwo Jima island, but he always had a sense that the U.S. had made Japan into what it is today. President Clinton, on the other hand, has been watching Japanese television sets and riding in Japanese cars since he was born. [To President Clinton], Japan has always been an adult."[38]

* * * * *

When Japanese and Americans first encountered each other in the mid-nineteenth century, they were deeply suspicious, even afraid of each other. But as would happen again when the U.S. Occupation forces arrived a hundred years later, after World War II, they soon found themselves getting along far better than they had ever dreamed. The Japanese admired the Americans for their openness, their good humor, and their technology. The Americans admired the Japanese for their arts and crafts, their esthetics, their discipline, and their politeness.

On a personal level, Japanese and Americans seem to get along remarkably well. There have been many uplifting instances of helping each other at the grassroots level, as when Americans sent aid to Japanese after the 1923 Tokyo earthquake or when Japanese sent aid to Americans after the 1906 and 1989 San Francisco earthquakes. But even in the depths of World War II, there were times when the lack of Japanese animosity to the United States was surprising.

On February 16, 1942, after Pearl Harbor and the fall of Singapore, the American ambassador to Japan, Joseph C. Grew, wrote in his journal, marveling that "In spite of all the war propaganda, there does not seem to exist any fundamental hatred of the United States among the people."[39] And he wasn't the only one to note this, as difficult an observation as it may have been when Japanese and Americans were slaughtering each other. During the war, John K. Emmerson, a Foreign Service officer who interviewed many captured Japanese soldiers in Asia, wrote in a report to his superiors, "When questioned about the United States and Americans, the Japanese prisoner seems to lack feelings of hatred or even personal animosity. On the contrary he often has heard of American wealth and attractions and has come into contact with American movies, jazz music and modern inventions and appliances. It's more familiar to him than any other foreign country. This explains his desire to go there after the war. Also, together with the good treatment, it explains his completely cooperative attitude. He volunteers to criticize propaganda leaflets, to write propaganda against his own troops, and in general help the American Army."[40]

The surprise was not just on the American side. After World War II, Japanese men, who had been told that they would be killed or castrated or exterminated as a race, and Japanese women, who feared they would be raped or enslaved, were almost universally awed by the magnanimity and friendliness of the conquering Americans. It is something for which older generations of Japanese still feel deeply grateful, and the feeling was reinforced by the return of the captured Okinawan islands to Japan in 1970. Even today, during the periods of rough relations that Japan and the United States regularly go through, when some Japanese talk disparagingly about the United States as though it were headed for the garbage can of history, they will often wax nostalgic in practically the same breath for the "good old days" when America was the undisputed leader of the world, and fervently hope for a comeback.

That we Japanese and Americans have had ups and downs in our relationship is clear. At times we have almost had a torrid love affair, and in one horrible period we even slaughtered each other. On the whole, however, ours has been a remarkably amicable relationship, characterized by friendship. And all the while we have steadily grown closer and closer. Will America and Japan someday fuse together and become a single entity? There are those who have suggested some sort of union. Former national security advisor Zbigniew Brzezinski, for example, noting that Japan and America produce 40 percent of the wealth in the world today, once advocated the creation of a special strategic and economic partnership called "Amerippon."[41]

This is not likely to happen. But even if it does not, America's and Japan's destinies are already linked. In a way we have become like a yin-yang symbol. Our societies are profoundly similar and profoundly different at the same time, existing in a complementary balance, intertwined within a subscribed circle. The differences cause tension, but also attraction, and hold out the possibility of extraordinary synergies.

TWO

Foe

*The struggle between Japan and the United States,
punctuated by truces, friendships, and brutality, will
shape the Pacific for generations.*

George Friedman and Meredith Lebard,
in *The Coming War With Japan*, 1991

*A*fter Commodore Perry arrived from America and forced an end to Japan's long isolation in 1853, one of the slogans of disgruntled samurai was *sonno joi*, or "Revere the emperor and expel the barbarians." Attacks on Americans and Europeans were not uncommon. Tokyo, wrote William Elliot Griffis, an American who arrived in Japan in 1870, was full of hundreds of patriot assassins "who thought they were doing the gods a service, and their country a good, in cleaving a foreigner in the street." About fifty foreigners, he noted, had already been killed since 1859, so that few "ever went far from their houses without [a revolver], and many wisely kept indoors at night, except upon urgent duty." After one attack, he described the mood of hysterical foreigners as a "nightmare of samurai, swords, blood, bleeding heads and arms, grave-stones, and grim death."[1] One of those slain in this period, in 1861, was Henry Heusken, the Dutch-speaking interpreter for the first U.S. consul to Japan, Townsend Harris.

The violence in the early years was by no means a one-way street. Many foreigners subscribed to a racial ideology that relegated Japanese to the status of uncivilized heathens, if not outright savages, and they responded to real or perceived slights with excessive force and demands for outrageous indemnities. Exaggerating only slightly, Griffis wrote that "a favorite threat of atrabilious Frenchmen, blustering Russians, and petty epaulet-wearers of all sorts, when their demands were refused, was to strike their flag, go on board a man-of-war, and blow up the native town. Yokohama still stands, having survived bombardment in five languages."[2]

Compared to other colonialist powers America adopted a more conciliatory posture toward Japan, but it was not above using force to resolve disputes or associating its interests with those of the European powers. In 1863, contrary to the provisions of a new treaty, a feudal lord in southern Japan closed the straits of Shimonoseki to foreign ships and fired on a U.S. vessel. In retaliation, a U.S. warship (with Joseph Heco, the first Japanese-American, on board as interpreter) sank two of the lord's ships. The next year, in 1864, a U.S. naval ship cooperated with European nations in an armed action against a Japanese fiefdom, attacking the daimyo's forts and forcing him to pay an extravagant indemnity.

The situation in Japan stabilized after a brief civil war and the establishment of a new centralized government hellbent on modernization. For several decades thereafter America and Japan got along splendidly. But the simmering misunderstanding and distrust with which the relationship began had set the stage for much greater problems.

Japan Gets Tough

Around the turn of the century, relations between Japan and America started to deteriorate. One reason was that Japan, in the process of trying to catch up to the "West" as fast as possible in all walks of life, had begun to emulate the worst qualities of Europe and America. For years the British, French, Dutch, and Germans had been carving up Asia much the way they did Africa, overthrowing indigenous governments and establishing colonies. Even America, despite its tradition of anticolonialism and a policy that favored keeping the independence of China, was not immune to the drug of imperialism. In 1898, after the Spanish-American War and acquisition of the Philippines, it, too, became a colonial power in Asia.

One of the driving forces behind Japan's modernization was a desire to avoid the fate of other Asian nations and the realization that this could only be done by importing technology, industrializing, and forming a strong military. But soon after modernizing its military, Japan began flexing its own muscles in the area. It went to war with China in 1894–95 and acquired Taiwan. Along with the Europeans and Americans, it participated in suppressing the antiforeigner Boxer Rebellion in China in 1900. And then, in 1904, in what marked a watershed in Japan's relations with the rest of the world, Japan went to war with and defeated Imperial Russia.

There were many causes of the Russo-Japanese war. Relations weren't helped by the fact that when Tsar Nicholas had toured Japan as a young man in 1890, he had been attacked and permanently scarred by a deranged, sword-wielding policeman. The biggest problem, however, was that Russia and Japan are geographical neighbors (separated by only twenty-six miles between the islands of Hokkaido and Sakhalin) and traditional rivals in their region of the Pacific. At the turn of the century, both Russia and Japan were in an expansionist mode, and both had designs on Manchuria and Korea. Japan, which had brutally invaded hapless Korea at the end of the sixteenth century and regarded the Korean peninsula as part of its sphere of influence, was particularly sensitive about what it considered foreign "meddling."

Perhaps out of traditional sympathy for the underdog, and a paternalistic protectiveness, American public opinion strongly backed the Japanese. President Theodore Roosevelt was an admirer of Japan, but did not want either it or Russia to gain too much power in the area. Writing in a letter to a British friend in March, 1904, he said, "It may well be that the two powers will fight until both are fairly well exhausted, and that then peace will come on terms which will not mean the creation of either a yellow or Slav peril." In a later letter he revealed a related fear. "I wish I was certain," he wrote, "that the Japanese down at bottom did not lump Russians, English, Americans, Germans, all of us, simply as white devils inferior to themselves [and treat us] politely only so long as would enable [them] to take advantage of our various national jealousies, and beat us in turn."[3] Roosevelt won a Nobel Peace Prize for finally negotiating a peace treaty between the two countries.

Japan's victory over Imperial Russian forces in the Far East set the stage for war between Japan and America. A small Oriental nation just emerging from a feudal past, whose generals had probably worn topknots and samurai armor in their youth, had trounced a very large "Western" power and challenged the belief of Caucasians in their own racial superiority. More ominously, Japan's victory had positioned it so it could later annex Korea while the rest of the world, including America, would merely acquiesce.

In Japan the war was enormously popular among the people. When the peace treaty mediated by Roosevelt was signed, crowds in Tokyo went on a rampage, angry that the war had been stopped. Victories over the Russians had been a salve on a national ego bruised fifty years earlier by the rude awakening from America and by the unequal treaties Japan had been forced to sign with America and the European nations. In reality, Japan was financially and materially near exhaustion from the war. Roosevelt's mediation and peace probably saved Japan from catastrophe, but the crowds were furious because they felt they had been unjustly deprived of further victories and the chance to obtain a huge indemnity from Russia.

Backlash

Relations between Japan and America emerged intact from the Russo-Japanese war, but they were quickly clouded by riots that broke out in California against the Japanese. At the turn of the century Japanese workers had begun to surge into the mainland United States seeking their fortunes like other immigrants, but a vicious backlash soon developed on the west coast, particularly in California, where people viewed the Japanese as competitors for jobs. Anti-Japanese agitation and attempts to limit immigration resulted, and after the 1906 San Francisco earthquake, groups like the "Exclusion League" advocated that all Asian children be segregated in public schools. These movements, when reported in Japan, caused an uproar among a proud people who felt they finally deserved to be treated on an equal basis with the more advanced nations, especially after their stellar performance against Imperial Russia. Like American newspapers, Japanese newspapers responded to the situation in an increasingly jingoistic fashion.

President Roosevelt considered the more troublesome California legislators "idiots" and had considerable sympathy for the feelings of the Japanese, but he was dealing with some of the most racist elements of white American society. In San Francisco (which today prides itself on its tolerance of diversity), Japanese restaurants were boycotted and Japanese residents (often referred to in the local papers as "little brown men") were attacked. After the San Francisco earthquake, despite the fact Japan had contributed more in relief funds than all other nations combined, a group of Japanese professors sent to investigate the damage was viciously stoned and assaulted.[4]

The immediate solution to the immigration problem was the so-called Gentlemen's Agreement, whereby Japan withheld the passports of laborers to prevent them from going to the mainland U.S. But the whole affair, with race riots and state-sanctioned discrimination (combined with the rapidly growing military strength of Japan in the Pacific region), so poisoned the atmosphere between the two nations that around 1907, when the media in both nations started reflecting and amplifying each other's jingoistic tendencies, talk of war became serious. Books with titles like *The Valor of Ignorance* and *Banzai!* in America and *Tsugi no issen* [The Next Battle] in Japan began appearing and predicting war. Rumors were rife. Roosevelt received reports from diplomats in Europe that the French and Germans were convinced Japan planned to attack. One report claimed the Japanese had secretly landed four thousand troops in Mexico in preparation for an invasion.[5]

Roosevelt's response, reflecting his "speak softly and carry a big stick" policy, was to send the entire U.S. fleet of battleships on an around-the-world cruise to Japan. Known as the Great White Fleet because the ships were painted white, it was far larger than anything Japan had. As Japanese author Naoki Inose has noted, one of the interesting things about this episode is that the Japanese political, corporate, and media establishment united to welcome the Americans. Newspapers printed banner headlines such as "U.S. Fleet *Banzai! Banzai! Banzai!*" Officers from the ships were wined and dined, treated like royalty, and cheered by thousands of schoolchildren waving American and Japanese flags. It was a grand display of friendship, yet only two weeks after the Great White Fleet departed the Japanese fleet sailed to waters southeast of Kyushu island where they conducted maneuvers with the U.S. as the assumed enemy. Although the visit of the U.S. fleet is largely forgotten in the context of the more dramatic events that later disrupted the U.S.-Japan relationship, it symbolized the direction things were going. "The war between Japan and America," Inose writes, "began with shared illusions formed in the wake of the visit of the Great White Fleet, in which both sides viewed each other across the Pacific as virtual 'enemies.' These illusions resonated with each other, and eventually led to real action—the attack on Pearl Harbor."[6]

The Road to War

From 1908 on, things slowly started going downhill. There was another war scare in 1913, with fears of a "yellow peril" fanned by the Hearst newspaper chain and also by the Germans trying to drive a wedge between the U.S. and Japan. Because Japan had formed an alliance with Britain during the Russo-Japanese war, however, in World War I Japan and the United States were de facto allies. Similarly, when an international force invaded the newly formed Soviet Union in 1918–19 (ostensibly to "protect" the trans-Siberian railway from the Bolsheviks), U.S. and Japanese forces again found themselves allied in action. But mistrust was building fast.

In 1924, the United States Congress adopted the race-based Immigration Act and unilaterally banned Japanese immigration. Many otherwise steadfast "friends" of America in Japan were infuriated. There had been another humiliation only a few years earlier, during the writing of the Covenant for the League of Nations. When Japan had proposed including a clause on racial equality, President Wilson, chairing the conference, had turned it down. Inazo Nitobe, a well-known champion of good relations between Japan and America and himself married to an American Quaker, later wrote of the Immigration Act that Japan "felt as though her best friend had, of a sudden and without provocation, slapped her on the cheek. She questioned the sanity of American legislators."[7] Baron Kentaro Kaneko, a close friend of Theodore Roosevelt and a fellow Harvard graduate who had worked hard from the Japan side to further U.S.-Japanese relations and to enlist U.S. sympathy during the war with Russia, indignantly resigned from the America-Japan Society, which he had been instrumental in forming.[8]

At the same time Japan was having problems with America, Japan was experiencing problems at home. Rapid modernization had created glaring social inequities. A huge gap existed between cities and countryside, not only in terms of standards of living but in social values as well. This produced a reactionary movement centered around the military, which increasingly rejected what it saw as Western "decadence" in favor of nationalism, emperor worship, and a return to *bushido*, or samurai values. In the 1930s, Japan's democratic institutions, which had been in existence only half a century, came under attack. Assassinations of political figures became common, and eventually the entire nation fell under the sway of the militarists.

Had this upheaval remained within Japanese borders, perhaps the United States would have been unaffected. But the Japanese military in effect hijacked the civilian government to further its own agenda, involving Japan in military incidents in Manchuria. These led first to the formation of a puppet state there and then to war in China in 1937. With modernization and medicine, the population of an already crowded Japan had doubled since the mid-nineteenth century, so the idea of more land, and of empire, was intoxicating. Success in turn bred arrogance and delusion among the nationalists, and a believe in the superiority of "the Japanese way."

To the United States, which stood for an independent China and had its own colony in the Philippines, the Japanese moves were disturbing and threatening. The sense of danger increased when Japan entered into a tripartite alliance with the European fascist powers, Germany and Italy, and started making moves into French Indochina. As the U.S. ambassador in Tokyo wrote in his journal on August 1, 1940, "The German military machine and system and their brilliant successes have gone to the Japanese head like strong wine."[9] The U.S. response was trade sanctions on the raw materials that Japan depended upon and an ultimatum that Japan withdraw. Japan's response, in a replay of a tactic used in the war with Russia in 1904, was the attack on Pearl Harbor.

The Japanese military mistakenly believed that America was a decadent nation lacking the "fighting spirit" and spiritual discipline of Japan, and that it would eventually settle for peace. What it did not realize was that the attack would cause an outburst of national anger that would coalesce into the greatest military force the world has ever seen, resulting in the utter destruction of Japan's military. By the time World War II ended, the United States had lost over a hundred thousand men in the Pacific area. Japan, which had been embroiled in war not only with the United States, but with the British Empire and Commonwealth forces, local resistance movements, the Chinese, and the Russians, had lost an empire and nearly three million people, and its cities were in smoking ruins. As American scholar John Dower has eloquently pointed out, for America the war with Japan was even more vicious than that with Germany because it was a race war, and "a war without mercy," in which both sides often didn't bother to take prisoners.[10]

The attack on Pearl Harbor was one of history's greatest military blunders. It is interesting to speculate what Japan's fate might have been had it decided not to attack Pearl Harbor but Russia instead, as many in the military advocated, or merely moved into the Southeast Asian colonies of England, France, and Holland. Would the isolationist American public, long fed a diet of anti-Soviet propaganda, have been willing to fight to save the Soviet Union, which had been cooperating with Nazi Germany? Would Americans, with their strong anticolonialist ideology, have been willing to die to defend European empires in Asia?

A New Type of Competition

Japan and America are no longer at war, although one cannot always tell this from the tone of public and private pronouncements in both countries. The competition that exists today, we should continually remind ourselves, is mainly economic and not military. There is a profound difference between the two.

After World War II, the United States remade many aspects of Japanese society in its own image. In the process it created the postwar parameters of the two nations' relationship. It provided for Japan's defense and gave it access to its huge, lucrative markets, while Japan remained America's faithful ally, allowing the U.S. military to use Japanese territory as a forward base against communism in Asia. If Japan did not always vocally support American foreign policy, it at least acquiesced to it in nearly all cases.

The United States encouraged Japan to prosper, and prosper it did, beyond anyone's wildest imagining. After being jump-started by the Korean War, Japan's economy developed such momentum that over the next several decades it went on to rival and even outperform that of the United States. To Americans today, deluged with news about Japan's new-found wealth and news about their own new-found economic problems, the question therefore becomes, is Japan merely an ordinary economic rival or is it a special threat to our national well-being?

At first glance, the idea that Japan could be a serious threat or even be doing anything "unfair" seems ludicrous. Consider a few of the enormous advantages the United States has in any economic competition:

- The United States has a land mass twenty-five times greater than Japan's and is rich in natural resources. The U.S. depends on imports for only around 18 percent of its energy, whereas Japan depends on imports for nearly 85 percent. And although on a per-person basis Japan's gross domestic product is larger than the U.S.'s, the total U.S. GDP is still more than 40 percent larger than Japan's.[11]

- The population of the United States is almost exactly double that of Japan, and soon will be younger and more vital. Because of slowing birthrates and longer life expectancies, Japan has the fastest aging population in the world; at current rates, by 2025 it will have nearly 10 percent more slowed-down, if not doddering, seniors than the U.S.[12] Unlike America, Japan cannot continually recharge itself with immigration.

- The common language of the United States—English—is the lingua franca of the world. Americans can often communicate with the rest of the world in their own language, whereas Japanese people, whose language is spoken only in Japan, must spend enormous time and money learning English and translating information.

- The United States has had a strong hand in establishing the international rules under which most trade is conducted today—such as the General Agreement on Trade and Tariffs (GATT)—and holds virtual veto power over an evolving new set of rules.

- The United States' ownership of the world's key currency (dollars) insulates it from many currency rate fluctuations; in a worst-case scenario, it could just print more money to pay off its dollar-denominated debts.

So what are we worried about?

The Occupation of America

If Japan seems particularly threatening to the average American, it is because in the last decade or so we appear to have been invaded. The components of this invasion are very familiar by now. Everything is "Made in Japan." Japan is buying too much U.S. real estate. Japan has too much leverage over our government because it has purchased so many of our treasury bills. Japanese factories are popping up all over America, "threatening" our economy. And Japanese lobbyists are exerting too much influence on our political system, pressing for the passage of laws that benefit themselves more than they benefit Americans.

Taken on an individual basis, however, are these trends threatening and are they really Japan's fault?

It may seem that everything is "Made in Japan," but the United States still manufactures a fairly high percentage of the goods it uses. Japan, however, makes increasingly more of the goods that we actually interact with in our daily lives—visible items like cars, VCRs, and stereo systems. No one forces us to buy these things. We purchase them because we want them, or, as is increasingly the case, because American manufacturers are unwilling or incapable of making them anymore.

Real estate purchases were particularly unsettling in the 1980s mostly because they increased so suddenly and in high-profile areas. This happened mainly because changes in currency rates and rapid appreciation made U.S. property very attractive to Japanese investors, and because Japanese firms are very status conscious, with a strong "herd instinct" that makes them imitate each other. By the early 1990s Japan was in recession, investment had cooled, and many cash-strapped American property owners were wistfully longing for the good old days. Despite fears of a "fire sale," the Japanese buyers may not have gotten very good deals. As the *Washington Post* pointed out in 1992, some Americans "are emerging as the wily horse traders while the Japanese appear to have been snookered."[13] Even if this had not been the case, selling land is a fairly safe way to raise money compared to selling technology or know-how. Real estate cannot be taken out of the country, it remains subject to local laws and rent controls, and if worse comes to worst it can always be nationalized.

Japan's purchase of a huge share of United States government debt has primarily been a reflection of the higher interest rates offered on U.S. government bonds (compared to Japan's) and their perceived security. For the U.S. government, with its desperate need of financing, the money has been a godsend. It may be legitimate to worry about Japan deriving too great a say in the affairs of our government (especially by threatening to withdraw investment), but at least we are being financed by a friendly nation over which we have enormous influence. And if this bothers us we could always try to reduce our budget deficit.

What about those new Japanese factories in America? It is true that they do not contribute as much to the national economy as American-owned factories; they repatriate much of their profit, may not use as many locally manufactured goods and parts, and may not allow locally hired people to advance to top positions. But they do bring important benefits. They provide employment to U.S. citizens and revitalize local economies, and because they have to abide by U.S. laws the "playing field" between Japanese and U.S. firms is made more level. And in areas where U.S. firms are technologically lagging, transplant factories provide an opportunity to see how Japanese do things, without our going to Japan or engaging in expensive industrial espionage. Since, unlike Japan, America has a highly mobile work force, many Americans who have acquired advanced on-the-job training at Japanese companies will wind up working for U.S. firms, and Japanese managers will become targets of American head-hunting, thus transferring an otherwise-hard-to-acquire body of knowledge.

Finally, Japanese lobbying is a real concern—but so is lobbying by the Arabs and the Israelis and even by the American tobacco industry. The most flagrant abusers of the system—the money-hungry U.S. officials who take high-paying jobs as lobbyists for Japanese corporations immediately after leaving office (as Ronald Reagan unhesitatingly did in 1989 when he performed $2 million worth of PR work for Fuji Sankei Communications)—may disappear beneath the scowl of public disapproval. The rest can be dealt with by legislation.

The truth of the matter is that in most of the areas where Japan seems threatening to Americans, Japan has merely been acting the same way the United States has acted toward other, far less economically powerful nations in the past. And Japan has been operating in ways our political and economic systems are designed to encourage. If there is something about this that we do not like, such as lobbying activities, or that we deem truly threatening to our national interest, the burden is on us to change our laws. If we feel our legislators are all bought off by Japanese corporations, the burden is on us to throw them out of office. We can hardly expect Japan to change its policies toward us unless we are willing to change ourselves.

Godzilla and the Trade Deficit

Even if much of the Japanese "threat" can be argued away, there are very real problems between Japan and the United States. Although the U.S. had to physically force Japan to trade with it in 1853, today the most divisive issue between our two nations is the fact that, since the beginning of the 1980s, we have been buying far more from Japan than we sell to Japan. The result, for the U.S., is a frighteningly large trade deficit of nearly $50 billion per year, with little prospect of improving soon.

Any serious discussion of the cause of this trade deficit, however, quickly becomes complex and confusing. It goes far beyond the emotional charges often hurled by Americans of protectionism on the part of Japan, or by Japanese of laziness on the part of American manufacturers and workers. Even the experts themselves sometimes sound like characters in Akira Kurosawa's classic 1951 film, *Rashomon*, where different people give wildly different versions of the same event.

One of the basic reasons for the deficit lies painfully close to home. Even if Japan did not exist, we would still tend to run a trade deficit with the rest of the world because of a decline in the rate of our savings, which is at least in part caused by our huge federal budget deficit. The federal budget deficit makes it hard to save money that could be used for investment, education, and a host of other things, and it forces us to import large quantities of capital so we can continue to live in the style to which we are accustomed. And because we are buying more things than we are selling, we have to "pay" for these things with the sale of our own assets—stocks, bonds, real estate, and even whole corporations.[14] In effect, we are selling off part of our future and in so doing we are actually creating many of the things described above that seem so threatening to us. And if we sell too many of our assets to Japan or any other nation, it is true that we will accomplish exactly what we fear most—the gradual loss of our political and economic independence.

The Argument over Reciprocity

If Japan and America were one nation no one would worry about the trade imbalance, any more than anyone worries about the trade imbalance between Hawaii and California. The imbalance would be offset by free flows of goods and people and by taxation, and since we would be using the same currency we would not need to earn foreign exchange. Because we are still separate nations, however, the problem transcends economics and becomes political. What keeps coming back and threatening to derail relations between us is not just the trade deficit, but the nature of it: its size, its intractability, and certain patterns in it raise the issue of reciprocity and the suspicion that Japan is not playing by the same economic rules we are.

Arguments over reciprocity started soon after the U.S. occupation of Japan ended. They have continued ever since. American government officials have complained to Japan about exports of toys, textiles, televisions, automobiles, computer chips, supercomputers, and telecommunications equipment. The charge was, and remains, that Japan protects its home markets, fosters its own industries through a variety of policy measures, and then, when its industries are strong enough, decimates targeted American industries by using a concentrated low-cost export drive to grab a bigger and bigger share of the market. The pattern is depressingly familiar now in ever more sophisticated industries, and so is the response. Trade representatives from both nations negotiate at great length and paper over the problem with an agreement of some sort. The Japanese government promises to open its markets and initiates a publicity program with catchy slogans designed to increase imports, or it launches a campaign to encourage overworked corporate warriors to take more vacations. The problem disappears from the front pages of newspapers for a while. And then, like Godzilla, it always comes back—bigger, and harder to ignore.

It is easy to see why many Japanese people have a confused, defensive reaction when their government is criticized for its trade policies and accused of not having an open market. One can almost hear a chorus of voices saying, "We import lots of American stuff—on a per-capita basis, even more than you import of our stuff. We're practically drowning in Marlboros and Coca-Cola and Levi's and U.S. movies. And besides, our postwar economic miracle has been based on working hard and manufacturing relatively inexpensive goods of high quality for sale on the world market, and what's wrong with that?" A free-trade, consumerist ideologue in the United States would agree. The American consumer, he or she would assert, only wins. This is the sort of reasoning that leads some Americans to consider the trade deficit a sign of strength, or, as Nobel Prize–winning Milton Friedman wrote in an article in 1993, that it is "good for the United States." Quoting Adam Smith, who stressed two centuries ago that the only true purpose of production is consumption, Friedman emphasizes the obvious fact that American consumers directly benefit only from goods and services that are imported, not exported.[15] What he de-emphasizes, of course, is that the imports have to be paid for.

And this is only one area where discussion of trade reciprocity and fairness gets very tricky. No nation has a positive trade balance with all of its trading partners all the time. And most trade statistics today only reflect trade in merchandise. Sometimes, as *Newsweek* noted in 1992, if services are added into the equation there is really hardly any trade deficit with Japan at all.[16] Finally, making things even more complex, is the fact that Japan, which lacks resources, naturally tends to concentrate its exports in manufactured goods so it can pay for the food and materials it needs.

Japanese are fond of pointing out that Japan today actually has less outright "protectionism" than many other advanced countries. Other than Japan's notorious ban on foreign rice (lifted only when massive crop failure occurs), there are relatively few laws on the books preventing imports. Nor are there many legal restrictions preventing foreigners from investing in Japanese industry or even buying Japanese firms. As if to illustrate how tricky direct criticism of Japan has become, in June 1992 Japan's Ministry of International Trade and Industry started releasing reports comparing the level of protectionism in Japan with that of its main trading partners. In the first report, covering ten categories such as government procurement practices and antidumping measures, Japan came out the best next to Singapore; the United States had the worst score of all.[17]

Were it not for the enormous sums of money involved in these arguments they would be rather comical. There are, however, some very disturbing patterns to Japan's trade and investment. First, Japan runs a trade surplus with nearly every major region of the globe (with the notable exception of Australia and the Middle East, on which it depends heavily for raw materials), and many of its trading partners have a high savings rate and no budget deficit. Second, even when the trading partner is an industrialized, high-tech nation like the United States, Japan still imports relatively few manufactured goods compared to the amount it exports, even in areas where it starts out with a major handicap, such as in semiconductors and telecommunications equipment. Third, and in the long run most disturbing, although cash-laden Japan is relatively free to pick and choose among the best American high-tech and knowledge-based companies to buy and add to its portfolio, and thus strengthen its high-tech capability, the reverse is not true. There may be few laws on the books in Japan today that outright prohibit United States companies from investing in or buying Japanese firms, but whether it is high cost, red tape, or cultural attitudes there are clearly some formidable nonlegal obstacles—foreigners control less than 1 percent of all corporate assets in Japan, compared with 20 percent in the United States.[18] These patterns may not be the result of a sinister plot and may instead stem entirely from a complex web of historical, cultural, and geographical factors. Nonetheless, the patterns do exist, and they are so pronounced that many people have claimed Japan's trade and investment policy resembles that of colonialist nations of the last century. Those European powers imported only raw materials and exported manufactured goods. In the case of Japan, some people have also charged, an additional export to its trading partners is unemployment.

Rethinking Japan

Starting in the 1980s, a noticeable shift occurred in the way many American opinion makers viewed Japan. Instead of regarding Japan as America's star pupil in democracy and capitalism (an "economic miracle"), more and more people began to worry that Japan might be operating under a very different set of assumptions about trade and national security, and that it might even be a threat to the American-created, postwar world order.

The main reasons for this shift were simple—the soaring U.S. trade deficit and accompanying economic problems; the late-to-bloom realization that Japan was not just a copycat nation, that in many areas its technology rivaled or surpassed that of the U.S.; and in the late 1980s the end of the Soviet threat and global communism as the the primary focus of normally Eurocentric American political and intellectual establishment.

Several incidents speeded the shift. In 1982 Hitachi was caught by an FBI sting operation in the process of trying to acquire industrial secrets from IBM. In 1988 a subsidiary of Toshiba was discovered to have sold sensitive military technology to the Soviets that jeopardized the security of U.S. nuclear subs (this resulted in the public smashing of Toshiba products in Washington, D.C.). And, in a popular off-the-cuff 1989 book titled *No to ieru Nihon* [The Japan That Can Say No], coauthored by Shintaro Ishihara, a politician, and Akio Morita, the founder of Sony, Ishihara suggested that Japan needed to assert its own interests more and that it might tip the global balance of power by selling its semiconductor technology to the Soviets.[19] When the U.S. Department of Defense's crude, unauthorized translation of this book was circulated among U.S. opinion-makers (accustomed to more deferential Japanese public figures), it created an uproar.

In the same decade, and not coincidentally, a new school of "revisionist" writers appeared who cast a critical eye on Japan's trade practices. In 1985 renowned journalist Theodore H. White created a stir with a vituperative article in the *New York Times* magazine titled "The Threat from Japan." In it he charged that America had been too nice to Japan after World War II, that Japan was now systematically dismantling American industry, and that Japan might have "won the war" after all. White was a member of the war generation who had personally witnessed Japan's surrender and had admitted not liking the Japanese, so perhaps his opinions could be written off as sour grapes.

Not so with some other very respected writers. Four of them—often referred to as the "gang of four"—achieved considerable notoriety. Chalmers Johnson, a political scientist, in 1982 wrote a study of Japan's Ministry of International Trade and Industry titled *MITI and the Japanese Miracle* that showed how this government agency had coached and directed Japan's industries to a degree unthinkable in the United States. Clyde Prestowitz, who had been a U.S. trade negotiator with Japan during the

Reagan era, in 1988 wrote *Trading Places,* a damning expose of how Japanese government and industry consistently managed to bamboozle American trade negotiators. James Fallows, Washington editor of the *Atlantic Monthly*, in 1989 wrote an article titled "Containing Japan" (the title hinting ominously of a threat equivalent to global communism), which argued that the Japanese economic system was incompatible with that of the U.S. and therefore must be contained. And finally, Karel van Wolferen, a respected Dutch journalist with over twenty-five years experience in Japan, wrote both in the U.S. magazine *Foreign Affairs* and in a scathing book titled *The Enigma of Japanese Power* that Japan was a nation without a political center, where no one was really in control.

In some circles in both Japan and the United States these men were accused of being "Japan-bashers," if not outright racists. In Japan—markedly paranoid about criticism from the outside—this sort of reaction was to be expected. In the United States the criticism came from "friends" of Japan and traditional "Japan-hands"—scholars and opinion-makers who hewed to the more orthodox line of thinking that regarded Japan as an economic miracle, a model student of America, or who had spent their professional lives trying to help Japan and America get along after the bloodshed of World War II. Many of them preferred that any criticism of Japan take place at a more rarefied level, for fear of arousing the very real, always-lurking-beneath-the-surface racist sentiment in America.

In reality, the gang of four was criticizing America as much as Japan, and many of their criticisms have been borne out by subsequent developments. The reaction to their writing was nonetheless so intense that they took the extraordinary step in 1990 of publicly defending their views (and their honor) in a joint article in *U.S. News and World Report*.[20] Titled "Beyond Japan-Bashing; The 'Gang of Four' Defends the Revisionist Line," this article heralded the polarization that exists today, in which Japan-observers are divided into camps of Japan-bashers and Japan-boosters (or what is variously called the "Cherry-blossom" or "Chrysanthemum" crowd) with virtually no middle ground left between them.

The real mystery is why Americans ever thought Japan and America were operating from a set of shared assumptions about trade. One can only blame it on distortions in our thinking caused by our long and drawn out ideological confrontation with the Soviet Union. A rich and successful nation, we were committed to a concept of "free trade" that we had defined ourselves, and we were willing to overlook a great deal in order to make sure that Japan stayed in the U.S. ideological camp. When the Soviet threat evaporated, the differences in our economic systems came into focus so fast we almost seemed to have been blindsided.

The Myth of Free Trade

Free trade is only an ideal. It means that trade between nations should be carried out unencumbered by restrictions, quotas, tariffs, and exchange controls. When free trade thrives, the theory goes, "comparative advantage" allows nations to specialize in what they do best, maximize their talents and their economies of scale, and reap the benefits. It seems to work best, however, between societies with a relatively similar economic and political structure.

Our trade with Japan today hardly resembles "free" trade, and in most cases has become poorly "managed" trade. On the U.S. side, industries such as steel, automobiles, semiconductors, and machine tools are all protected today because we have pressured Japan to "voluntarily" restrain its exports or to expand the share that such U.S. goods can obtain within the Japanese market.

On the Japan side, most of the obstacles to free trade today are subtle, nontariff barriers. Some of the flimsier arguments Japanese have given to explain why their government or society restricts certain imports are now legendary—for example, the claim that foreign skis don't work on Japanese snow or that Japanese intestines are too long for American beef. But it really only takes a look at the streets of Tokyo to realize that the biggest trade barrier is the very different structure of the Japanese economy.

With the removal of many formal trade barriers in the 1980s, sales of manufactured foreign goods in Japan have zoomed but not nearly as much as they theoretically should have. The value of the yen has nearly doubled against the dollar in the last ten years, so Japan should be practically drowning in imports, and much of the trade imbalance should have been automatically corrected. Yet most imports (and even many Japanese-manufactured goods) are still far more expensive than in the United States, and consumers, instead of rioting, have scarcely protested. With the high cost of Japanese labor one would also expect imports of low-end cars to increase, just as sales of Volkswagens and Datsuns increased in the United States in the 1960s. But while sales of foreign cars in Japan have increased dramatically, almost all are European luxury cars like Mercedes and BMWs; one can drive all day through the streets of Tokyo without encountering a Korean Hyundai. And a walk down those same streets reveals thousands of tiny bars and shops staffed by one or two people but with almost no customers, and small businesses with some customers but lots of employees—all establishments that would go out of business overnight in the United States.

Some of these things can be explained by Japan's Byzantine distribution systems; by corporate groupings and stock cross-holdings that tend to keep out outsiders (and encourage what would be called collusion in the United States); by land-use policies and taxation systems designed to help small businesses; and even by corporate ethnocentrism. It might be tempting to assume this is all a grand conspiracy against the outside world, but reality is more complex. One reason there are so many books being written about the Japanese system is precisely because there are so many things about it that are not yet properly understood—in either the U.S. or Japan.

The point is that Japan's form of capitalism is different in many ways from that of the United States. Considering that Japan developed completely outside the Judeo-Christian tradition and was totally isolated from the rest of the world for nearly two hundred and fifty years, why shouldn't it be? Some writers describe Japan's economy as "producer-oriented" as opposed to "consumer-oriented," or as "market-share oriented" instead of "profit-oriented." Chalmers Johnson calls Japan a "capitalist developmental state." Economist Lester Thurow and others refer to it as a "communitarian" state. One American author, Douglas Kenrick, even wrote a book on Japan titled *Where Communism Works*. Whatever the nomenclature, as Japan has developed a system that is increasingly efficient at spitting out new products in exports, the United States has developed a system that is increasingly efficient at sucking them in as imports.

Some Remedies Old and New

The question then becomes, what can the United States do? We can start, of course, by putting our own economic house in order, by cutting our federal budget deficit, by increasing our savings and investment, and by making our industry more competitive. But that will take political will and great pain. And it will take time. Such measures will only help incompletely, of course, if part of the problem is also the structure of the Japanese economy. To remedy that, we can work on a multilateral basis, as we have historically, to expand free trade with all our trading partners under the umbrella of GATT. In recent years, however, these talks have nearly broken down because of our disagreements not just with Japan, but with the European Community. We can continue to devalue the dollar against the yen, which makes our goods more competitive and easier to export. But the dollar has already declined from ¥360 per dollar in 1970 to nearly ¥100 per dollar in 1993, and devaluing the dollar means that we Americans earn increasingly lower wages relative to our competitors. Finally, we can resort to overt protectionism and impose restrictions on imports, or we can try to force Japan to change its system.

Of these alternatives, the last, which is now the one being pursued most aggressively, is the most problematic. It consists not only of pressuring Japan to abandon its tradition of protecting select agricultural industries (such as rice) and to tighten its intellectual property laws (like copyrights). It also pressures Japan to change its distribution system from one supporting mom-and-pop stores to one encouraging chain stores, and to alter its real estate policies to bring down the cost of land and thus correct one of the most obvious distortions in the Japanese economy.

To do this we have been negotiating within the context of the Structural Impediments Initiative and applying direct political pressure in a kind of good-cop, bad-cop routine. The president and his representatives, acting very sympathetic to Japan, ask the Japanese government to make changes. If Japan doesn't change, they warn, it will be impossible to control the U.S. Congress (which is already clamoring for protection for U.S. industry), and Congress will pass laws restricting Japanese imports. Fearing loss of the markets that have allowed it to acquire such enormous wealth, the idea goes, Japan will be moved to compromise.

Most of the demands the U.S. makes on Japan are in the best interests of the Japanese people, and especially the Japanese consumer. But in many instances (such as land use) they are also a request for Japan to change its social system, which in any other context would be regarded as a gross interference in the affairs of a sovereign state. The Japanese call this *gaiatsu* or "external pressure," and view it in the same light they viewed the changes forced upon them by the arrival of Commodore Perry or the U.S. Occupation Forces. In Japan today, *gaiatsu* is used by the political establishment both as a tool to institute difficult reforms without taking responsibility for them and as a way to unite the nation—and it is so taken for granted that in April 1993 (in what must be a historical first for the leader of an independent nation) then Prime Minister Miyazawa even publicly declared external pressure necessary.[21] But it also serves to reinforce growing Japanese impressions of the Americans as a bunch of overbearing, arrogant, whining losers, trying to promote poor-quality products no one wants. And it will also encourage Japan in the future to make demands on the U.S. to change *its* system—the exact scenario many Americans fear most.

Getting Personal Again

U.S.-Japan relations follow a regular cycle today. Long tranquil periods, when the media of both nations are preoccupied with other issues, are punctuated by crises. During the crises attention is brought full bore on old problems, but nothing is resolved.

A recent low in U.S.-Japan political relations occurred around the end of 1991. Japan had incurred the resentment of many Americans during the Gulf War when, instead of participating directly in the fighting, it merely donated money (that Japan was prohibited from fighting by its constitution was a point lost on most Americans, who understandably wondered why they had to risk their lives for the oil that Japan needed). Later in the year the news media in both nations had a feeding frenzy over the fiftieth anniversary of the attack on Pearl Harbor, increasing tensions all around. Aggravating things further, some irresponsible Japanese politicians began making disparaging remarks about U.S. workers and minorities. Then, in January 1992, when an exhausted and ill President Bush took some leaders of U.S. industry to Japan in a high-power, high-pressure attempt to win further trading concessions, the result was frustration for Japanese and humiliation for Americans. Instead of meeting the best of U.S. industry, the Japanese found themselves being alternately lectured and begged by overpaid U.S. auto executives, whom they could hardly listen to with much respect. And when an overly exhausted George Bush attended a high-level banquet, Americans were treated to the televised spectacle of their ill president vomiting in the lap of Prime Minister Kiichi Miyazawa and collapsing on the floor.

Some U.S. politicians tried to capitalize on American frustrations. At a rally of factory workers Senator Ernest Hollings of South Carolina suggested that his audience remind the Japanese people that it was American workers who had once made the atomic bombs dropped on Japan.[22] In the U.S. popular press, where ominous images of the Rising Sun had graced the covers of news and business magazines for years, but mainly to symbolize an economic threat, a new image of Japan began to appear. More and more novelists portrayed Japan as a threat to U.S. security, much as the Soviet Union and Communism had once been portrayed. In Michael Crichton's best-selling book *Rising Sun*, and later in the toned-down, confused movie, the Japanese were depicted as crafty, omniscient, almost all-powerful manipulators. In the same period racial attacks on Asians in the United States also started to increase.

Thinking the Unthinkable

The notion of another real war between Japan and America seems absurd. Most government and industrial leaders don't talk about it, like guests at a dinner party who are expected to keep the conversation civil. But when tensions rise, it is a possibility on everyone's mind.

A nonfiction book called *The Coming War With Japan* appeared in 1991. In it, the American authors analyze recent trends from a strategic standpoint and determine that profit-oriented U.S. corporations are incapable of competing with growth-oriented Japanese corporations, but that the U.S. must nonetheless bring its trade into balance with Japan. Despite the best intentions of both nations, they claim, Japan will rearm to secure its position in the Pacific, and the U.S. will be tempted to use its military and political power to restrain Japan. War will result. But that's not all, for the "struggle between Japan and the United States, punctuated by truces, friendships, and brutality, will shape the Pacific for generations." It will be an endless war, they say, "the war of all against all."[23]

In the Japanese media, both domestic and international economic competition have long been treated as a form of warfare. There are whole genres of books and magazines that do nothing but compare the business strategies of corporate executives to those of great samurai warriors or World War II military figures. In this environment, in a nation with a near-neurotic obsession about how it is viewed by the outside world, books like *The Coming War With Japan* fit right in. While selling 40,000 copies in its first nine months in the United States, it reportedly sold 60,000 copies in three weeks in Japan.[24] And, of course, it also spurred the publication of Japanese books with titles like *Nichibei gunji shototsu no kozo* [Structure of the Military Clash Between Japan and America], written by a Japanese but deliberately subtitled, in English, "Coming War with USA." As tensions rose in 1992, one major Japanese newsweekly noted how, on subjects like the "decline of the West" and "criticisms of America," the writings of some Japanese (including the "Japan That Can Say No" politician Shintaro Ishihara) were starting to sound more and more like the writings of nationalists right before World War II.[25]

Change Is in Both Our Interests

Ultimately, the economic friction between the United States and Japan will lessen when the United States puts its own economic house in order and tailors its free-trade, laissez-faire ideology to the reality of a world where different nations have very different economic structures and very different goals. Much of the trade tension will also diffuse when we recognize that the difference in the structure of our economies produces economic problems, not only with Japan but with a host of other newly developed states, as well as with a united Europe. As Japan's plummeting stock market and the recession of 1992-94 showed, Japan will not always be as economically successful as it has been in the past. And as the improvement in quality of U.S. manufactured goods has shown, U.S. industry is not yet ready for the dustbin of history.

Japan, for its part, will have to change even more than America, or risk impaling itself on its own intransigence. Japan is, after all, the biggest beneficiary of the postwar free-trade system and through it has peacefully achieved what it once failed to gain through war. As Sony's Akio Morita noted in an interview in 1993, Japan has a problem. "We [Japanese] talk about a borderless world," he says, "but Japan still has borders. Unless Japan's economy can be integrated into that of the world, we will not be able to survive." Like more and more thinking Japanese in both industry and government, Morita is a strong advocate of opening Japan's markets and negotiating a new set of rules for international trade so it can be played like a sport—with fierce competition, but without malice and resentment.[26]

One of the great ironies of the trade problems between Japan and the United States is that both nations find themselves in similar dilemmas. The United States needs to reduce its deficit to increase savings and competitiveness, but voters have become so used to the benefits of deficit spending that reducing the deficit is unbearably painful to contemplate—even though not doing so will bring ruin. In Japan, the structure of the economy needs to be changed, but in its current form it has enriched people's lives so much that the idea of change is terribly traumatic—even though not doing so will jeopardize the entire world trading system.

Eventually, we will muddle through our trade problems, the Japanese market probably becoming more consumer-oriented and open, the U.S. market probably becoming more producer-oriented and closed. Unfortunately, trade is not the only issue threatening to derail the relationship between Japan and America.

The Defense Dilemma

In 1951, the United States and Japan concluded a security treaty. The treaty was extremely unequal, designed to provide for defeated Japan's defense but really a pretext for U.S. forces to remain in Japan. Japan had little say in how the U.S. forces would be used; since the Occupation was just ending it was hardly in a position to protest. In 1960 the agreement was revised to a slightly more equal Treaty of Mutual Cooperation and Security that spelled out a mutual desire to "strengthen the bonds of peace and friendship traditionally existing" between the two nations and "to uphold the principles of democracy, individual liberty, and the rule of law." Economic cooperation was listed as a goal. Again, however, the

United States committed itself to defend Japan, while Japan was under no obligation to defend America.[27]

In Japan, opposition to the revised treaty was intense. After its total defeat in World War II, many Japanese had developed passionate pacifist beliefs, and many feared the treaty would entangle Japan in an American-initiated war with the Soviets or result in more pressure to rearm. Others simply were offended by the continuing large presence of U.S. bases on Japanese soil. Unlike today, where trade problems are something intellectuals, politicians, and bureaucrats worry about, a broad-based, intensely emotional protest movement developed in Japan. Prior to ratification of the treaty, huge demonstrations by students, labor, ordinary citizens, and housewives snarled the streets of Japan's cities. President Eisenhower had planned to visit Tokyo to commemorate the treaty and sent his press secretary, James C. Hagerty, in advance to make preparations. When the poor man arrived on June 10, 1960, his car was surrounded by thousands of angry protestors and he had to be rescued by a U.S. military helicopter. The treaty was rammed through Japan's parliament, but Eisenhower never did make it to Japan.

Japanese people have learned to live with the security treaty, and even to realize its benefits, but they remain deeply skeptical of the military in general, whether the U.S.'s or their own. Since the 1950s, the U.S. has therefore been in the ironic position of not only defending its former enemy, but constantly prodding it to beef up its own armed forces. U.S. politicians and officials still gripe that Japan is getting a "free ride" and not doing or paying enough for its own defense. As recently as October 1992 the Pentagon released a report claiming that Japan's contribution to U.S. and allied defense was "substantially below par."[28]

There is no question Japan's relatively low defense burden gives it a competitive economic "advantage" over the U.S.—it frees resources for investment in more productive areas, such as industry. But with the collapse of global communism as a threat, encouraging Japan to spend much more on defense becomes extremely problematic.

As of 1992 Japan was subsidizing U.S. troops on its own soil to the tune of $4 billion a year. Under U.S. pressure Japan had increased its defense budget so that in dollar terms, while still under 1 percent of total GNP, it was one of the world's largest next to that of the U.S.[29] It had also eliminated the long-standing taboo against deploying its forces overseas. By 1993 gun-toting members of the Japanese military were patrolling with the UN peacekeeping forces in Cambodia, and five civilian Japanese policemen had already died in action. Further pressure on Japan to undertake more of its own defense, or to pay the U.S. more for providing it, therefore plays into the hands of the powerful Japanese right wing and raises the disturbing specter of a fully rearmed Japan. It is a prospect that still unnerves neighboring nations that were invaded by Japan in World War II. And it threatens to make an utter farce out of Japan's constitution.

Japan's constitution was authored in 1946 by Americans, whose hand is betrayed by the "translation-ese" of the Japanese used in the document. It is masterly and idealistic, drawing heavily on U.S. experience in government and guaranteeing Japanese people rights previously denied them (such as women's right to vote). Since, after World War II, it was U.S. policy not only to democratize Japan, but to permanently defang and demilitarize it, the constitution also reflects this. In English, Chapter II, Article 9 states:

> *Aspiring sincerely to an international peace based on justice and order, the Japanese people forever renounce war as a sovereign right of the nation and the threat or use of force as a means of settling international disputes.*
>
> *In order to accomplish the aim of the preceding paragraph, land, sea, and air forces, as well as other war potential, will never be maintained. The right of belligerency of the state will not be recognized.[30]*

This "peace" constitution was enormously popular with the average Japanese, but shortly after it was promulgated the global struggle with communism began. The U.S. was placed in the embarrassing position of having to reverse policy and encourage Japan to partially rearm after all. The Japanese government reluctantly complied, using various semantic machinations such as the name Self-Defense Forces to legitimize the military and declaring that it could only be used in nonaggressive roles.

Today it is imperative that Japan revise the 1946 constitution soon—particularly the defense clause—for three reasons. First, although the constitution is popular among Japanese, it is not actually Japanese, which means that the Japanese right wing (and left wing) will always be able to attack it as "foreign." Second, if the constitution were rewritten soon, public opinion would probably insure that the new version adhere to the original, if not to the letter at least in spirit, and allow Japan to retain the high moral ground it currently enjoys. Third, the more the words and the spirit of the constitution are violated, the more it will cease to have any meaning whatsoever. Even a third grader can tell that the SDF is blatantly in violation of the constitution as currently written.

New Roles in a New World

For relations between Japan and America (and the rest of the world) to be truly normalized, and for Japan to assume a role on the world stage commensurate with its economic status, many ghosts of World War II will have to be put to rest. The United Nations Charter, which still lists Japan as an "enemy nation," will have to be revised, and Japan will probably have to be given a permanent seat on the Security Council. The treaty with the U.S. will also have to be revised soon to put Japan on a more equal footing in terms of both rights and responsibilities.

There will be strong resistance to such moves in Japan and the U.S. The current defense arrangement and the general disengagement of Japan from world politics has functioned well until now (and brought Japan many economic benefits). People within and without Japan will fear the motivations of those making the revisions, and dread the specter of rearmament. But the changes will have to be made anyway because the U.S., with its huge federal and trade deficits, is hardly capable of subsidizing wealthy Japan's defense. Nor, with the collapse of the global communist threat, will the U.S. be able to politically justify maintaining so many bases in Japan. The only real rationale for a U.S. presence in Japan today is as a stabilizing force in Asia and a guarantee against Japanese militarism. Under the security treaty there are fifty-five thousand U.S. troops stationed in Japan to "protect" it,[31] but there should be no mistaking their other, unstated role: they are also, as Marine General Henry C. Stackpole, a divisional commander on Okinawa, said in a frank interview in 1990, "a cap in the bottle, if you will" against an armed, resurgent Japan.[32] At some point, however, more and more Japanese will ask themselves why they should pay anything for someone else to protect them from their own excesses.

The Ghosts of History

At the beginning of the 1990s the blunt prime minister of Singapore, Lee Kuan Yew, was widely quoted as saying he didn't want Japan to become involved in UN-style peacekeeping operations because it could be "like giving liqueur chocolates to an alcoholic."[33]

Why be afraid of Japan? This is a serious question, because not only foreigners, but many Japanese themselves regard the future of their nation with some trepidation. This is not because the Japanese are by nature a warlike people; based solely on the number of wars it has been involved in over the last four hundred years, Japan ranks among the world's most peaceful nations—especially when compared with the European powers or the United States, with its own short but bloody history. Nor are people afraid of Japan simply because Japan has such enormous economic clout. Part of the concern stems, one suspects, from decisions made by the United States at the end of World War II. And part of it is certainly due to the inherent structure of Japanese society itself.

When the U.S. dropped atomic bombs on Hiroshima and Nagasaki in early August 1945, the bombs hastened the end of the war. But they were used in an act of indiscriminate slaughter and overkill, leaving horrible radiation-induced aftereffects in many survivors. They were, as the emperor said in his surrender announcement, "a new and most cruel bomb." The bombs encouraged many Japanese to view themselves as "victims" of the war, thus allowing them to ignore the atrocities and suffering Japan itself had inflicted on neighboring nations. This victim-persecution complex has indirectly helped insure the survival of some disturbing, usually unstated, subcurrents in Japanese thought.

One notion is that the Pacific War was really a war to liberate Asia from the colonialist European powers. While the war had that effect, whatever good intentions Imperial Japan had were canceled out by behavior even more atrocious than that of the colonialist powers. And China, which Japan invaded, or Korea, which Japan annexed, were never European colonies in the first place.

Another notion is that President Franklin Roosevelt and the United States "tricked" Japan into attacking it to facilitate U.S. entry into the war with Germany. This belief is bolstered by conspiracy theories still floating around America and Europe. In hindsight it is still hard to understand how the U.S. military could possibly have ignored the warning signals. (On January 31, 1941, Joseph P. Grew, the U.S. ambassador to Japan, even noted in his diary that Tokyo was abuzz with rumors of an attack on Pearl Harbor and that he had informed his government.)[34] As seductive as such conspiracy theories are, however, they still do not alter the fact that it was Japan that initiated hostilities.

More disturbing is the belief that World War II was a plot by white foreign powers to deprive Japan of its rightful destiny, and that this same conspiracy continues today in the economic realm.

Is the Emperor System a Black Hole?

Japan is hardly the only country that prefers not to dwell on its mistakes. The United States is still struggling to come to terms with its role in Vietnam, after all. But neighboring Asian states still view Japan with suspicion at least in part because Japan has inserted watered-down descriptions of its World War II role in its school textbooks and because Japanese leaders have rarely made forceful apologies. When the young, progressive politician Morihiro Hosokawa became prime minister in August 1993 in an election upset, he took the dramatic and welcome step of apologizing publicly and profusely, but his apology is not the one many people are waiting for. Every time the Japanese emperor visits Japan's former enemies, his words are carefully analyzed by the Japanese and host nation media, and every time the words get closer to a true apology, yet still gingerly tiptoe around becoming one.[35]

This problem has been exacerbated by a decision made at the end of World War II. Despite war-crimes trials of military men and extensive purges throughout the Japanese government, the U.S.-led Allies decided to retain Emperor Hirohito in power. This was clearly a wise move at the time, since it made the occupation and governing of Japan infinitely easier. But like the dropping of the atomic bombs, it made the assignment of responsibility for the war more difficult. The official line is that although the emperor was a "living god," he had no political power during the war and thus was unable to control the militarists who seized power. The other side of the coin, however, is that retaining the emperor in power eased everyone else's collective responsibility because discussion of responsibility automatically became a very sticky subject—how can one discuss national responsibility without discussing the emperor's role? In 1990 when the mayor of Nagasaki suggested that the late Emperor Hirohito was partly responsible for the suffering of Japan in World War II, he was shot and nearly killed by a right-wing attacker. In 1992 the right wing of Japan was vehemently opposed to the new Emperor Akihito visiting China; they were afraid he would be compelled to issue a demeaning, official apology.

Most Japanese have little awareness of their emperor today—far less, say, than British subjects have of their queen. And because they have little direct connection to him, the idea that he might have any influence over them seems rather absurd. Prior to 1945 the emperor was regarded as a "living god," but the very first article of the first chapter of the U.S.-authored Japanese constitution carefully relegates him to a ceremonial role similar to that of European monarchs:

The Emperor shall be the symbol of the State and of the unity of the people, deriving his position from the will of the people with whom resides sovereign power.[36]

In his 1986 book *Mikado no shozo* [A Portrait of the Mikado], Japanese author Naoki Inose ponders what French philosopher Roland Barthes wrote upon visiting Tokyo for the first time and seeing the huge imperial plaza in the center of the city. Barthes said, "While Tokyo does possess a center, this center is empty." "Perhaps," Inose comments, "to Japanese, in their pell-mell race for ever greater efficiency, it is a convenient symbolic space, a giant black hole that swallows all disputes."[37]

Inose was speaking in a positive sense, implying that the emperor system has little power today but that its existence nonetheless provides a sumbolic focus for Japanese society. He is certainly right. The present emperor himself is a fine, decent, and very modern man legally demoted by the constitution to a figurehead role. But the emperor system really represents the continuation of the old system; it is a symbol, not only of the nation and the unity of its people, but of a great deal of feudalistic and mystical mumbo-jumbo that ought to make people from democratic societies like the United States rather nervous. Just as Japan's huge surpluses with its trading partners symbolize how its economic system differs from that of other nations while at the same time resembling them, the emperor system symbolizes how Japan's political and social system, while appearing very "Westernized," is nonetheless very different.

The emperor of Japan occupies a position fundamentally different from that of any monarch in European history. With a traceable lineage supposedly going back over a thousand years (over 2,600 years if one believes the legend), his racial purity has in the past been linked to the myth of Japanese racial purity. He was also, prior to World War II, considered a living deity; even today he has a far closer connection to the Shinto religion than most Japanese like to admit. In Europe, linking the racial purity of monarchs to that of their subjects was never remotely possible, because international marriages were conducted as a form of diplomacy and monarchs were often of different ethnic origin. Nor, in the Christian hierarchy, could European monarchs ever have been elevated to the level of a living deity, unless they were willing to risk excommunication, universal condemnation, and the possibility of being violently dethroned. In fact, one of the biggest differences between the emperor of Japan and the head of nearly every nation in the world that has enjoyed a monarchy or an imperial system, including England, is that the people of Japan have never had the luxury of deposing their ultimate leader.

The Social System

Almost alone among modern nations, Japan has never experienced a true social revolution. Japanese people have undergone enormous political and social change, but this has almost always been in reaction to outside pressure and led by the elites, in one form or another. The core establishment has been rearranged and reshuffled, as in the Meiji Restoration of 1868, or during the U.S. Occupation, but never entirely overthrown.

One result is that many vestiges of feudalism remain. An example is Japan's special organizational dynamic. Japan looks like a vibrant, modern democracy and a nearly classless society—its four-tiered hereditary caste system of farmers, warriors, craftsmen, and merchants was abolished over a hundred and fifty years ago. But a strong emphasis on hierarchy remains in the language people use with each other and in the way they interact.

Almost all group relationships in Japan, but particularly those in male-oriented organizations, are categorized and prescribed by seniority and status, and are held together by a sticky web of obligations and responsibilities. The group relationship is one of the great strengths of Japanese society; it makes possible an awesome solidarity in clubs, schools, workplaces, and, as in World War II, the military. When the social dynamics work as they're meant to, individuals can achieve a sense of belonging and security that most Americans will experience only in fraternities, sororities, neighborhood gangs, churches, or their immediate family.

But for this harmony individuals pay an enormous price. Japanese people are not the faceless, humorless robots they are sometimes portrayed to be in the U.S. media. In small group situations, however, the subtle forces that can be brought to bear on individuals to conform, to observe a myriad of social rules, are tremendously powerful. This is not a genetic or racial trait; when an American truly fluent in Japanese is speaking Japanese in an organizational environment, he or she will feel the same pressures. It is an integral part of the culture, and strongly linked to language.

For example, if two Japanese businessmen who have not been introduced to each other are in a room together, it is very difficult for them to speak to each other, even if they desperately want to, because they don't know each other's status and thus don't know what level of formality and honorifics to employ in their speech. Or at a meeting of two Japanese men who are otherwise wild individuals, freelancers, freethinkers, and bohemians, if they have ever been members of the same organization before they will revert to a standard pattern of relating to each other. Even if nearly the same age, they will relate as seniors and juniors, the junior using the appropriate patterns of deference and respect, the senior demonstrating his seniority and his kind concern for his junior.

This is one reason so many Japanese artists and freethinkers want to leave the comfort of their homeland for places like New York or Los Angeles. This is also one reason many early Japanese immigrants to the U.S. quickly learned to mix the hierarchy-neutral English pronouns "me," "you," etc. in with their Japanese speech; instead of saying, "*BOKU wa genki desu, KIMI wa?*" (I'M fine, how about YOU?), they say "*ME wa genki desu, YOU wa?*" Constantly thinking about hierarchy in speech and behavior and constantly trying to conform to social expectations can be an extraordinary psychological burden.

And in group situations, it can also make it extraordinarily difficult to say no. Politician Shintaro Ishihara, in his book *The Japan That Can Say No,* pointed out the need for Japanese to become more assertive and to express their true feelings in their dealings with foreign nations. But what he did not stress enough was that Japanese also need to express their opinions more forcefully within their own groups. Although rarely mentioned, this is surely one of the main reasons foreigners often view Japan with unease—Japanese people are so obsessed with hierarchy and group harmony that they are often not very good at openly and forcefully expressing disapproval or dissent.

The result is a tendency to vicious factionalism in Japan. If it is difficult to dissent alone in one's group, the logical thing to do is to find like-minded dissenters and form a new group. It also breeds the loyalty conflicts that are a staple of Japanese Kabuki plays, samurai movies, and modern soap operas. But in the real world loyalty conflicts cause real trauma. Millions of Japanese (and other) lives were needlessly lost in World War II because people couldn't say no to their superiors, all the way up to the emperor, when the nation was obviously going to lose. Even today, the media are filled with stories of people of all classes who cannot bring themselves to say no within their group, or of groups that won't let members say no; of company employees who, not wanting to disappoint their superiors and unable to turn down absurd requests for overtime, work themselves to death; and of schoolchildren, because they are "different" from their peers, who are harassed to the point of suicide.

The Small-Group Dynamic

Japan today enjoys great pluralism in its media and its intellectual culture. Its people are arguably more peaceful and more antiwar than in any other nation. Why, therefore, should anyone worry about a group dynamic of the sort that exists in Japan? The answer is that it means at least one mechanism for a terrifying degree of social control still survives, should anyone attempt to unite all the factions and small groups that are still at the basis of Japan's pluralism. Outright coercion is not necessary to enforce conformity in Japan; the fear of being ostracized or left out of whatever is the mainstream fashion or fad is usually enough.

Japanese comedian Beat Takeshi liked to poke fun at the reluctance of many Japanese people to jaywalk across streets alone when the light is red, even at three in the morning when there are no cars in sight for miles. "It won't be scary," he'd say, "if we all cross together." Around 1986, when the color white became fashionable in Japan, 70 percent of the passenger cars pouring out of Toyota factories were white, with the figure as high as 90 percent for some models.[38] Asking consumers why, one would get answers ranging from "it's a clean color," to "white cars have a higher resale value."

But Japan's social dynamic is not always so amusing. It is one of the reasons corporations can force so many employees to "work too hard," as even hardworking Japanese themselves often lament. The historian Saburo Ienaga once noted how efficiently the populace was manipulated on a mass level in World War II. Noting that Japan, unlike Germany, never had any true concentration camps and almost never had executions for treason, he writes, "Strangely enough, this may only mean that oppression was actually greater in Japan. Every aspect of life was so regimented and controlled that no one could plan a treacherous act worthy of the death penalty!"[39]

Political Stasis, Political Rot

There are many signs that this same social dynamic has made Japan's democracy dysfunctional. People vote and go through the motions of democracy, and there is great public debate over issues, but the end result is something unlike the democracy Americans know. For nearly forty years, from 1955 to 1993, Japan was ruled by various factions of one party—the LDP, or Liberal Democratic Party. Vocal opposition parties, including the Communists, Socialists, and others, existed, but they were weak and ineffective. In many areas such as consumers' rights, the United States, with its constant nagging at Japan's government to liberalize its markets, took over their role. As a result of the security pact, the U.S. has also de facto handled most of Japan's foreign policy for the last half century.

In the postwar period this virtual single-party system provided enviable political stability and an opportunity for enormous economic growth. But with this stability came an abdication of political responsibility, political stagnation, and corruption. One series of scandals followed another, and a growing scorn of politicians in general spread among the populace. The pattern was always the same. The media would delight in exposing a prime minister or cabinet minister who had taken bribes or illegally used funds; the accused person would resign and apologize, posts would be reshuffled, and then it would be back to business as usual.

All that seemed to change in the general election of July 1993. The fed-up electorate finally delivered the LDP a slap. A rickety coalition of eight parties became the "ruling party," and the LDP went into opposition. This was heralded as a great political revolution around the world, but on close inspection the big winners in the election were still the traditional conservatives. In the coalition, the reformist parties that had gained the most votes were composed mainly of former LDP men; the head of the coalition, Morihiro Hosokawa, was himself a former LDP member. In an *Aera* magazine poll of the electorate conducted only days after the election, the vast majority of the respondents indicated dissatisfaction with the results. Eighty-two percent, including many who had voted for LDP parliamentarians, felt the LDP had won too many seats in parliament.[40] It was doubtful the new coalition could remain in power long. The LDP, in one form or another, would probably come back stronger than ever. And either way, the level of political rot in the existing system presented a formidable obstacle to substantial reform.

A political scandal that erupted in 1992 illustrates the problem. A tiny extreme right-wing organization, the Kominto, or "Imperial People's Party," had been harassing the head of a major LDP faction (who later became prime minister) by loudly and publicly praising him, thus causing him embarrassment. In order to pressure the group to stop, the aging Shin Kanemaru—a shadow LDP "kingmaker"—enlisted the help of a moving company with ties to organized crime. At some point, somewhere between ¥2 and ¥3 billion (between $16 and $24 million) exchanged hands, in cash. As one newsmagazine marveled, in bills this amount of money would weigh 660 pounds; if stacked in boxes, it would be nearly 100 feet high.[41]

This episode was only the beginning, for when Kanemaru's house was searched, investigators found around $50 million in cash, securities, and gold bars. This scandal shows how large the power vacuum is in legitimate Japanese politics, and the enormous power a small number of tiny but fanatic right-wing groups can wield. Right-wing groups such as the Kominto are increasingly staffed by former gangsters, or *yakuza*, so that the line between them and organized crime has begun to blur. Other than by their greed and desire for power, they are united mainly by their self-appointed mission to preserve traditional (especially semifeudal and hierarchic) Japanese values, and, above all, to protect the emperor. The emperor is virtually invisible and supposedly powerless in Japanese society (a "black hole," as writer Inose might say), but, historically, whoever has controlled the emperor has controlled the nation.

Most Japanese are disturbed, even embarrassed, by their nation's political problems. The real question is how the problems will be resolved.

Will a new coalition reform Japan? Will the scandal-racked Liberal Democratic Party reform itself? Or will reactionary forces step in? Reacting to the swirl of political corruption, a Japanese major in the Self-Defense Forces shocked the nation in October 1992 by suggesting in a high-profile article that the military should be used to overthrow the civilian government. "The only means left [to correct injustices]," he wrote, "is revolution or a coup-d'état." He was quickly and correctly cashiered, but he may not be the last person to make the suggestion.[42]

A Unique People?

The Japanese right-wing—the self-appointed guardian of the emperor and the nation—is the crystallization of a troubling subcurrent of thought that runs through mainstream Japanese society. This is the belief that Japan is a unique nation and that the Japanese are a unique race of people with a semimystical role to play in history.

Every nation likes to think that it is unique, and indeed, every nation is unique. But in Japan this is carried to extremes. Traces of this belief appear in nearly every conversation with a foreigner at some point, usually indicated by the exclusionary phrase *Wareware Nihonjin wa*, or "We Japanese people are . . . " and then plunging into absurd generalizations about why 125 million Japanese people are intrinsically different from all other people on earth, or why they do this or that in such and such a unique way.

The theory of uniqueness is closely linked to the myth of racial purity, and both are reflected in the enormously popular genre of literature called *nihonjinron* ("Theories of Japanese-ness") or *minzokuron* ("Volkism"). Books in this genre explain why Japanese logic is different from "Western" logic, why Japanese brains interpret the sounds of insects as music, and on and on. The result is a type of schizophrenia, where many Japanese people on the one hand assert their uniqueness but on the other hand crave the assurance that they are really not unique—that they are part of the human race, members of the community of advanced nations, and not completely isolated in the world.

This same schizophrenia is symbolized by a large body of popular books and articles that see the world in terms of Jewish conspiracies or use flow charts to show how U.S. policies are controlled by Rockefellers or Zionists bent on destroying Japan. These same anti-Jewish books are counterbalanced by admiring, pro-Jewish books that attempt to show how the Japanese and the Jews are really similar (creative, hardworking, possessing few resources, ostracized in the world). One of the first and most famous works in this genre, *The Japanese and the Jews*, was written in 1970 by Shichihei Yamamoto, who pretended to be an Israeli named Isaiah BenDasan. Today positive books on Jews have multiplied into a subgenre of literature that attempts to claim, like the book *Nihonjin no ruutsu wa yudayajin da* [The Roots of Japanese are the Jews], that Japanese people actually *are* Jews. Others, such as *Nihon no naka no yudaya* [Jews in Japan], attempt to analyze Japanese folk songs and find hidden "Hebrew" words in them. Most of these are fringe books, but they result from the same overemphasis on uniqueness. Ultimately the Jews are only a metaphor for a basic insecurity about the outside world.

For Americans, the Japanese belief in uniqueness has immediate implications. It clashes directly with the U.S. ideology of equality, diversity, and universality, and smacks of racial arrogance. And it means even constructive criticism of Japan can be difficult. Careless criticism, such as attacks on Japanese trade practices or political policy, quickly creates a "circle-round-the-wagons" attitude that makes any negotiation very difficult. In the publishing world, since Japanese love to read praise and criticism of themselves by foreigners (both reinforce the sense of uniqueness), a large market for books in both categories exists. Pat Choate's 1991 book *Agents of Influence* was a critique of Japanese lobbying in America. A Japanese publisher reportedly paid $270,000 just for the translation rights.[43] With figures like that, it is not surprising that there has been a boom in highly irresponsible and critical books written by foreigners and slapped together for sale only in Japan. No wonder many Japanese readers think the whole world is out to "bash" them.

· · · · ·

It is easy to criticize another nation and even easier to make it a scapegoat for the problems at home. That is not the goal of this book. If this book were for Japanese people, it would focus on the structural problems in U.S. society that make Americans difficult to get along with. It would present the sordid history of racism. It would question whether the U.S. is a true democracy (do the American people elect their president, or does the electoral college?). It would even postulate that the United States is a volatile, warlike, jingoistic nation with a thin veneer of civilization, neurotically obsessed with being "No. 1." And many Japanese readers would nod their heads in agreement.

But this book is not for Japanese. It is for Americans. Despite Japan's enormous similarities to the United States, there are aspects of its culture that are still very different. Differences need not always cause conflicts, but unless properly understood they will always make conflicts more likely to occur. Trade is the biggest issue between our nations now, but it may be the easiest to solve. Other issues may be more difficult. How, for example, will Japan arrive at a defense role that it, the U.S., and the rest of Asia feel comfortable with? How will America, for that matter, contend with a Japanese technology policy that aggressively promotes nuclear power and has a strong nationalistic component?

As Americans it is not our business how the Japanese want to organize their society or run their political system—until it affects us. Then, when we work together to try to solve common problems, the subcurrents in Japanese thought—such as the widespread belief in "uniqueness" coexisting with a persecution complex, the organizational dynamics of Japanese society, the dysfunctionality of Japan's political system—all become obstacles. And all are interrelated. Japanese people want desperately to reform their own political system, but the same sticky, hierarchical human relationships upon which their society is still built make engineering any reform extremely difficult.

Will the United States and Japan go to war again? Probably not. We need to keep the relationship in perspective, after all. The United States has gone to war with all sorts of other nations in its short history, including twice with Britain, but never over trade issues. Our relationship with Japan, for all its problems, is far more secure than Japan's relationship with South Korea, Taiwan, Russia, and even China, all countries with which Japan has outstanding territorial disputes. The real challenge for the United States and Japan will be to negotiate around the shoals in the relationship without antagonizing each other and without encouraging the forces of darkness in each other's society—especially now that the media in both countries increasingly conduct a blitzkrieg approach to the issues of the day. In Japan, the emperor/power-vacuum and the right wing are always lurking in the background. In the United States, the forces of racism and jingoism are always simmering below the surface.

The relationship between Japan and America is held together by a fragile harmony of interests. Should reactionary or racist forces ever assume power in both nations at the same time and try to make scapegoats of each other, or should both nations begin to resonate out of synch again, the result would be a catastrophe.

THREE

Model

Why can't America be more like Japan?

Title of an article by Edmund G. (Jerry) Brown Jr.,
in *California Magazine*, 1985

*W*hen the fog of the Cold War finally lifted at the beginning of the 1990s, many Americans found their hard-won victory over the Soviet Union to be a rather hollow one. As at least one U.S. politician put it in 1992, "Japan won."

While the quality of life in America slips, our own media seem to delight in reminding us that Japan has lower unemployment, crime, and infant mortality rates; greater average longevity and per-capita gross national product; and higher academic and even (most painful) average IQ scores. Today it is Japan—our enemy-turned-emulator, our once-mocked supplier of cheap consumer goods—that we increasingly measure ourselves against, and fall short of. Both at home and abroad, more and more people who used to study American ways of doing things now study Japanese ways of doing things. Increasingly, it is Japan, not America, that is the world model.

Our Love Affair with Japan

When Americans first encountered Japan in the mid-nineteenth century, they were fascinated. After its long isolation, Japan seemed extraordinarily unusual and mysterious, and easy to romanticize or "exoticize." The latter generally took two forms—the cultural and the chronological. In the first, Americans marveled over Japan's different customs, fashions, and arts. In the second, they saw a land unsullied by industrialization, a sort of pre-modern Shangrila with personal codes of honor, a sense of community, and even a spiritual purity that the West had lost long ago. As Earl Miner pointed out in his 1958 book, *The Japanese Tradition in British and American Literature*, Japan was an easy target for this sort of thinking, in part because it already had a fairly high level of civilization. It would have been far more difficult, he notes, "to exoticize or idealize the forms of Ubangi culture—or the Indian or the Chinese hinterlands—beyond a certain point, since few westerners can really imagine themselves happy for a moment in such societies."[1]

The most blatant exoticizing usually stopped as soon as Americans actually set foot on Japan's shores, but not always. Lafcadio Hearn, one of the great turn-of-the-century romanticists who had a lifelong fascination with the weird, the exotic, and what he called the "ghostly" aspects of life, arrived in Japan in 1890. Shortly thereafter he gushed in a letter to a friend, "I love their gods, their customs, their dress, their bird-like quavering songs, their houses, their superstitions, their faults. We are the barbarians! I do not merely *think* these things: I am as sure of them as death. I only wish I could be reincarnated in some little Japanese baby, so that I could see and feel the world as beautifully as a Japanese brain does."[2]

Unfortunately for Hearn, although he lived in Japan the rest of his life and even became a Japanese citizen, he was doomed to frustration. He arrived in love with a Japan that was fast disappearing and may never have existed in the first place. The more he saw Japan "Westernize" in dress, architecture, and spirit, the more depressed he became. In 1894 he wrote to another friend asking, "What is there, after all, to love in Japan except what is passing away?"[3]

Thus began the "Lafcadio Hearn Syndrome." For Americans who waxed romantic over Japan without ever having been there, or who lived there but never learned enough Japanese to completely understand what was going on around them, Japanese culture was covered by an opaque veil on which they could project whatever romantic fantasies they wished. And then, when the veil dissolved, disappointment invariably set in. William Griffis, who arrived in Japan some twenty years before Hearn, was one of the first to identify the problem. When European-style newspapers were started in Japan, he noted in his typically blunt fashion, they had quickly "exposed the fact that in these isles of the blest, in which some foreigners supposed existed only innocence, gentleness, or good-mannered poverty, reeks every species of moral filth, abomination, crime, and corruption."[4]

Today the Lafcadio Hearn Syndrome has by no means disappeared among Americans who become involved with Japan. There are those, usually unable to tolerate different diets and lifestyles, who have a visceral, negative reaction to Japan from the moment they set foot in the country. At the other end of the spectrum are those who fall passionately in love, and see in Japan everything they feel is lacking in America. These sentiments may last for months or even years, but after a lengthy sojourn, the pendulum swings, and as the visitors learn more of Japan's language and understand more of its culture, they find themselves in a love-hate relationship, loving Japan one day, and hating it the next.

Given enough time, most people reach an emotional equilibrium, and realize that Japanese people, as William Griffis concluded, are "simply human, no better, no worse than mankind outside."[5] Others, fantasies rudely destroyed, develop an overt dislike and distrust of Japan. While continuing to live there, they find themselves hanging out with other disillusioned foreigners, grumbling about this or that trait of the Japanese people, and, if they are Caucasians unaccustomed to being a minority, complaining about how "racist" Japanese people are. As a rule of thumb, the higher the expectations and the more inflated the fantasies of the visitor to Japan, the greater the later sense of ultimate disillusionment and even betrayal.

Changing Tastes

What is admired about Japan tends to go in and out of fashion. President Theodore Roosevelt once wrote his friend Kentaro Kaneko: "It seems to me, my dear Baron, that Japan has much to teach the nations of the Occident. Certainly I myself hope that I have learned not a little from the fine Samurai spirit, and from the ways in which that spirit has been and is being transformed to meet the needs of modern life."[6] Yet only a few decades later, when the American military occupied Japan after World War II, one of the first things they tried to eradicate was elements of the samurai spirit, banning martial arts and censoring comic books, movies, and novels. Children in school, carefully holding ink-soaked brushes, were directed en masse to black out offending portions of their textbooks.

Not too long ago many Americans admired Japanese people for their love of nature. Japan is abundant in natural beauty, and before industrialization generations of its people lived close to the land. They developed a rich natural vocabulary and a powerful connection to many of the microcosmic aspects of nature; these live on today in fond references to nature in poetry and letters and in a love of bonsai plants and haiku. In recent years, however, as Japan has experienced the same excesses of industrialization as other nations, in the American mind the image of Japan the pristine nation of nature lovers has been increasingly supplanted by an image of urban polluters, "whale killers," and corporate destroyers of the rain forest. In reality, Japan is less of an eco-criminal than the gas-guzzling United States; it has joined the ranks of other energy-hungry industrialized nations and in so doing disappointed a lot of people who had an overly romantic image of it in the first place.

In the 1950s and 1960s many Americans became attracted to Japanese spiritual traditions. Some found, and still find, Japan an excellent place for a spiritual quest. Others, however, found in Japan not a lofty spirituality but a bewildering mix-and-match, whatever-works approach to religion, with people paying lip service to both the Shinto and Buddhist faiths, getting married or practicing their English at Christian churches, and in public declaring themselves atheists. Those Americans who became involved in organized Japanese religions frequently discovered an emphasis on a feudalistic hierarchy, commercialism, and "this-worldliness" surpassing that of their native faiths.

In the late 1970s and 1980s, as Japan started to flex its economic muscle, American interest in Japan broadened beyond cultural issues. The U.S. political establishment was still obsessed with the Soviet Union and Europe, but more and more academics and businessmen began noticing how Japan was beating the pants off America in the global marketplace and solving many modern problems that we were still struggling with.

Already, in a 1970 book titled *The Emerging Japanese Superstate*, futurologist Herman Kahn had predicted Japan's economic success by extrapolating from its roaring growth rates. But it was not until 1979 that Harvard professor Ezra F. Vogel wrote the seminal book on Japan as a model, *Japan as Number One: Lessons for America*. Vogel suggested that Americans could learn much from Japan's approaches to government, company organization, education, welfare systems, crime control, and even—as incredible as it seems from today's perspective—politics. As if to symbolize what a radical notion this was at the time, the very upright former ambassador to Japan, Edwin O. Reischauer, borrowed a little drug terminology and proclaimed in a blurb for Vogel's paperback that "the very title will blow the minds of many Americans."

One of the first areas Americans emulated was Japanese business management. Just as books on American business management had once been the rage in Japan, during the 1980s a flood of books on Japanese management appeared in America with titles like *Theory Z* and *The Art of Japanese Management*. They sold mainly to American managers who were hoping, one would assume, to be able to motivate their employees to work like the Japanese. Unfortunately, many of the early books were also filled with gross generalizations, reflecting the long tradition among Americans of focusing on the form, or superficial aspects, of Japanese culture instead of the inner workings.

There is no question that many Japanese management techniques can be exported. Japanese manufacturers have solidly demonstrated this by setting up successful operations in the United States. Also, many American firms have successfully implemented the common-sense ideas espoused in books on Japanese management (such as having the bosses eat every once in a while in the same cafeteria as their employees) or the proven methodologies of quality control. But when American firms have tried to implement certain management concepts that have been very successful in Japan, like Total Quality Management, differences in corporate structure have led them into a thicket of problems.[7]

Focusing on white-collar workers in Japan as a model for American managers, moreover, was especially ill advised. As James N. Aliferis, the former head of the Japan Society of Northern California, and a consultant to high-tech industries exporting to Japan, noted in 1993, "The view that Japanese business management techniques are a model for nonmanufacturing areas has largely been debunked. Most people have realized by now that Japanese white-collar management is one of the least productive on earth. The lack of progress in office automation is an example. Beyond the need to build a consensus, the way the office is run is a disaster."[8]

On close inspection, the typical Japanese corporate office is staffed with too many people doing too little, with *madogiwazoku*, or the "sit by the window crowd," whom the company cannot fire because of its so-called lifetime employment traditions. Computers are used, but inefficiently, and often by OL, or young "Office Ladies," whose job it is to input data for older male employees who never learned to type and can't be bothered doing so now. And what looks like "hard work" often turns out merely to be inefficient work—hours logged to build a consensus in drawn-out meetings, to supplement a low basic wage with lucrative overtime payments, or simply to give the appearance of working hard. A joke among some Americans who deal with Japan is that one reason Japanese white-collar workers take so few holidays is that if they were gone for more than a couple of days it might be obvious how little work they actually do.

Today, Japan's economic success feeds the temptation to regard it as a model in ever broader fields, and it causes cracks to appear in the confidence most Americans have historically had in their own economic system. The shift in attitude has been so complete that when *Fortune Magazine* ran an article on "Japan's Influence on American Life" in 1991, it quoted a U.S. Toyota worker who had come back from a training mission to Japan. "'From how good they're doing,'" she felt obliged to note, "'you almost expect the Japanese to be superior people—but they're not different, really.'" "Perceptions like hers," the author of the article added, "are priceless because they imply a responsibility to measure up."[9]

Wishful Thinking

Often the very things Americans would most like to emulate about Japan are the most problematic. Nearly every visitor to Japan has a story to tell about the lack of graffiti and public vandalism, the politeness of the people, or a lost wallet returned the next day with its credit cards, travelers' checks, and cash untouched. For American women in particular the ability to walk alone through city streets late at night is invariably an exhilarating experience. Since a low crime rate permits an extraordinarily civilized life, it would be nice if we could import Japan's safe streets, if not its social order.

There is much for U.S. law enforcement experts to learn from Japan. L. Craig Parker, Jr., who wrote *The Japanese Police System Today*, concluded among other things that America needs national standards for police. He even claims that much unnecessary violence takes place in America simply because so many policemen are overweight and out of shape and thus more insecure and easily drawn into confrontations.[10] The most important thing America is learning from Japan, however, is surely the importance of good police-community relations. San Francisco, for example, has incorporated Japan's *koban* system of police boxes, or neighborhood stations, as a way of integrating the police into the local communities. Manned by at least two policemen in densely populated areas, these simple outposts provide a deterrent to criminals and friendly information and assistance for citizens.

But Japan's low crime rate depends on far more than hardworking, athletic police and *koban*. Many Japanese people, and even foreigners, attribute it to racial homogeneity—ignoring the fact that during large chunks of their history Japanese people were busy slaughtering each other; that at various times in the postwar period the streets of Japan have been filled with pickpockets, striking workers, and rioting students; and that in recent years some of the worst cases of social disintegration have taken place in racially and culturally homogeneous nations like

Cambodia and Somalia. In reality, Japan's modern social order has been maintained by equitably sharing sacrifices and the fruits of good economic growth, by emphasizing social consensus and community solidarity in a crowded environment, by a relatively upright police force, by strict handgun control, and by a process of socialization with not always benign origins.

Preserving the Social Order

Shortly before his death Lafcadio Hearn hinted at a greater realization of the complex roots of the graciousness and good behavior of the Japanese people he so admired. "Such manners" he wrote in 1904, "need not cease to charm us because we know that [they] were cultivated, for a thousand years, under the edge of the sword."[11]

During the Edo period (1600–1867), when Japan was isolated from the world for over two hundred years, a nearly flawless system of totalitarianism developed that permeated society all the way down to the neighborhood level. Social order was enforced by, among other things, a rigid caste system that gave samurai the right to lop off the head of any farmer or merchant they didn't like; laws that dictated even what color underwear townspeople could wear; a vast spy system that Joseph Heco, the first Japanese-American, called "nearly perfect"; and neighborhood social units such as the *goningumi*, or "five man teams." The *goningumi* were originally formed of village households by the feudal authorities to help stamp out Christianity and control masterless samurai, but they developed into a means of encouraging shared community responsibility and solidarity and of controlling society at the grassroots level. Outright feudalism was abandoned in Japan long ago, but it lives on today in social hierarchy and organization. In nearly every factory and school in Japan, there are units called *kumi* and *han*, where responsibilities are diffused among the members much as they were in the old *goningumi* system. One could even make a case for saying that the success of modern industrial

Japan is due in part to the grafting of feudal traditions onto a modern corporate structure.

Little overt coercion is required to maintain the social order today because most people instinctively know their limits. Unlike the United States, with its wide-open physical and intellectual spaces, there is nowhere to hide in crowded, island Japan. "Individualism," instead of having the heroic connotations it does in America, can still be a pejorative word, with shame a weapon to enforce conformity. Family registers maintained by the authorities provide a means of tracking the population and maintaining address files, and have been used by corporations to screen out minorities and "undesirables." Neighborhood vigilance groups and the ubiquitous signs advising citizens to call the police if they see "anyone looking suspicious" keep a damper on deviant behavior. And to exert control over the extra-legal elements of society, the authorities indirectly rely on the experts themselves—organized crime.

One of the great secrets of Japan's social order is the symbiotic relationship that exists between the authorities and organized crime. In an unstated agreement with the authorities, the *yakuza* (now officially called *boryokudan*, or "violent groups") have historically been allowed to maintain limited control over huge industries such as gambling, the sex trade, and even building construction. In exchange, they have cooperated with the authorities in maintaining public order by putting down leftist demonstrations (in the 1950s and 1960s), breaking up strikes, making sure their own criminal activity is largely out of sight and not disruptive to the general population, and even delivering the worst criminals to the police.[12] This cooperation may exist to a certain extent in nearly all countries, including the United States, but, as American authors David Kaplan and Alec Dubro observed in their 1986 book *Yakuza*, in few nations has organized crime existed so openly. *Yakuza* maintain public offices, proudly wear badges of gang affiliation, and even issue newspapers and magazines. Investigators at the U.S. Department of Justice were shocked in the mid-1970s when they discovered that Japan, despite its crime-free reputation, had nearly ten times the estimated number of gang members as the U.S., relative to population.[13] Recent crackdowns on organized crime may only drive it further underground and worsen the crime rate.

All this is to demonstrate how problematic the Japanese model can be. We Americans can learn a great deal about crime control from Japan, but we will never be able to import the Japanese system; nor would we want to, for Japan's low crime rate is achieved at a social cost that most of us would probably find unacceptable. For most of our crime problems, we will have to forge our own solutions.

The Industrious Japanese

Although a little over a hundred years ago many Americans complained about how slow and lazy the Japanese were, a 1992 survey indicated that the quality we now most admire about them is their "industriousness."[14] In the media this admiration is reflected by ceaseless use of the word "hardworking." In corporate suites the language is often more blunt. Off the record, American executives often express the wish to trade their fractious and ornery, union-dominated employees for a more "cooperative," "motivated" Japanese work force.

Most Japanese do work hard, but it is easy to confuse working long hours and faithfully singing company songs with working efficiently. As noted above, many hours are logged for the sake of appearance. And we forget that there is no particular merit in "working hard" per se. The goal of people everywhere should be to do as much quality work as possible in the shortest time possible, *with the least amount of effort*—that is, to be as productive as possible. One of the benefits of modern civilization is that we can use technology and tools to work less "hard" than our ancestors did and enjoy much greater rewards.

This misunderstanding of work has led to some damaging stereotypes and myths on both sides of the Pacific. Most Japanese seem to think they work harder than Americans, and many Americans seem to agree with them—a view that American management, for obvious reasons, would probably like to encourage. Yet at the beginning of 1992, after several Japanese politicians made some inflammatory remarks about lazy U.S. workers, studies came out which revealed that American workers' productivity was considerably *higher* than that of their Japanese counterparts.[15]

The other side of the coin is that long hours and hard work, especially on the factory floor, have often been squeezed out of workers in Japan using methods few Americans would want to adopt. Again, overt coercion is rarely required. Manipulation of small group dynamics by companies can create a one-for-all, all-for-one atmosphere, fostering a fear of letting down one's comrades, of disappointing one's group's superior, or of being ostracized. This is essentially a glorification of the traditional Japanese ethic of *messhi hoko*, or "annihilation of the self for the general good." Satoshi Kamata, one of the foremost critics of Japan's organizations, has noted that manufacturing employees in Japan often fail to report injuries during safety campaigns for fear of harming the corporation's record. The growing Japanese social phenomenon of *karoshi*, or "death from overwork," he also notes, is at least partly attributable to the sense of obligation employees feel, not just to work, but to attend endless work-related weddings, funerals, and drinking parties.[16]

The Japanese government—and probably no government has ever done this before—has been actively encouraging workers to spend less time at their workplaces, promoting five-day work weeks (instead of five and a half or six), and even rewarding cooperative firms with a special "Mellow Company" award.[17] One result, however, has been a boom in what is euphemistically called "service overtime." Employees feel pressured to work overtime by their companies but also pressured not to record the overtime hours to save their bosses embarrassment. It is a phenomenon caused—as *Aera* magazine noted in 1992 in an article somewhat harshly subtitled "The Pathology of Sheep-style Organizations"—by "excessive labor-management cooperation."[18]

Dangerous Generalizations

If there is a single mistake Americans consistently make in regarding Japan as a model, it is to overgeneralize about a very complex nation. We often assume, for example, that Japan's educational system is better than our own. Yet many Japanese people regard their basic education system as a competitive monster gone berserk, forcing children into endless rote memorization and after-hours cram schools, depriving them of the chance to develop independent and creative thinking skills. Universities, for that matter, are often merely places to recuperate from the pressures of high school and "examination hell," to engage in club activities, sports, and marathon mahjong sessions, and to learn how to socialize before making a long-term commitment to a corporation or a marriage.

The same overgeneralizations apply to the Japanese workplace. Even knowledgeable Americans often make glowing references to Japan's system of "lifetime employment," ignoring the fact that it is merely an ideal, and not a reality. Only around 15 percent of the Japanese work force, perhaps around the same percentage as in America, have enjoyed lifetime employment.[19] Smaller companies never offered it, and larger corporations have only "guaranteed" it with a long list of conditions. It has been predicated on high growth rates and on being male; "lifetime" has only meant until around age fifty-five; and when a corporation needs to "rationalize" and get rid of an employee, he may be given a demeaning make-work assignment, forced into a "voluntary resignation," or loaned for years to a subsidiary to toil in situations where firing would be preferable. When JNR, or Japanese National Railways, was privatized in 1987, many burly train drivers and ticket punchers found themselves working in restaurants or flower shops.[20]

Overgeneralizing about Japan is dangerous, too, because it can lead to severe under- or overestimations of Japan's abilities. This has happened in regular cycles since the mid-nineteenth century. Prior to World War II, many Caucasian Americans, convinced of their own racial superiority, believed Japanese forces could never be a match for European or U.S. military might. After Pearl Harbor, the ordinary Japanese soldier was overnight transformed into a superman. On the West Coast, people assumed Japan could strike them at will, and in a classic case of mass hysteria, antiaircraft batteries in California opened fire on imaginary Japanese attackers. The same pattern continues on a lesser scale today. During the late 1980s, many Americans perceived Japan's economy as an invincible juggernaut, about to take over the world. Then when the Japanese economy stumbled in the early 1990s, many were quick to write it off as finished. Reality usually lies somewhere between the two extremes.

Part of the problem is our lack of knowledge about a complex nation, and part of the problem is our subconscious tendency to indulge in the same sort of mythologizing that the Japanese do. In Japanese discourse, a considerable gap is tolerated between *tatemae* (surface appearances and intentions) and *honne* (true situations or true feelings). In general conversation, especially with foreigners for whom it is important to maintain a good impression, many Japanese people will make outrageous generalizations about themselves. These range from how Japan is a poor, tiny island nation with no resources filled with good-for-nothing people, to how Japanese has lifetime employment, virtually no crime or homosexuals, no trade barriers, and intrinsically superior aesthetics. Japanese people themselves may even believe the statements they make, for sometimes they may be true—on the *tatemae* level of discussion.

Is There Nothing to Learn from Japan?

Americans over the years have been fascinated by Japan precisely because there is so much to learn from it. Japanese culture being unlike European and American culture, Japanese approaches to a variety of modern problems seem refreshingly different.

But it is not just modern Japan that is worthy of our study. Ancient Japan, which still survives, slumbering under the veneer of modern life, has much to offer as well. Zen Buddhist and Japanese animist traditions can help bridge the Judeo-Christian dichotomy between man and nature and contribute to a truly ecological worldview. Japan's well-documented period of isolation in the Edo period provides invaluable lessons about the limits of trying to maintain political and social stasis as well as economic self-sufficiency. One of the shortest but most interesting books on Japan, *Giving Up the Gun*, written by American Noel Perrin in 1979, examined how Edo-period Japan effectively abandoned using guns and reverted to swords for two hundred and fifty years, speculating on how this experience might be applied to disarmament in the nuclear age.

Modern Japan, too, is a treasure chest of good ideas for Americans. Hungry tourists quickly realize this at street level—baffled by the Japanese language and writing system in restaurants, they find they can order by pointing at plastic food replicas, faithful down to the number of decorative green peas garnishing the plate. Many tourists also find out how comfortable and sanitary is the custom of removing one's shoes inside the home. In 1988, American author Leonard Koren introduced some of the more clever concepts coming out of Japan—the "Why didn't we think of that?" sort of thing—in his book *283 Useful Ideas from Japan*. Among the ideas was a water-conserving toilet with a sink on top where hands can be washed with the water that replenishes the tank after flushing, and prerecorded announcements on buses that announce local stops using not just station names but local landmarks.

Enterprising Americans are already busy incorporating Japanese innovations, ranging from sing-a-long *karaoke* bars to "dry beer" technologies, to soon-to-be-introduced "debit" phone cards. On the factory floor, American manufacturing engineers are busy applying the philosophy of *kaizen*, or "continuous improvement," and JIT, or "just in time" inventory control. The ideas of Japanese quality control "gurus" such as Shigeo Shingo and Genichi Taguchi have also gained a devoted following. Of Taguchi, one American expert gushed in 1988 that his method "quantifies common sense. The concept is going at Mach 1 through the auto industry."[21]

Benchmarking

Sometimes ideas from Japan may not be properly understood when implemented in America, but it may not even matter. There are plenty of American firms that have adopted Japanese quality control and management techniques without fully grasping their basic concept—and claimed to have gotten enormous boosts in productivity anyway. Merely reexamining one's business structures and manufacturing processes seems to help.

In the same way, the broader generalizations we make about Japan can be useful, since they help us establish new frames of reference and specific goals. A common observation by Americans is that it is easy to understand why Japan has become such an economic success by looking at the way clerks carefully wrap packages for their customers. Daigaku, the American Buddhist monk quoted earlier, claims that one secret of Japan's success is the Zen-based recognition that "nothing is important and that everything is important. That each part of our life requires care and attention."[22] A San Francisco artist in love with Japanese popular culture claims that one of Japan's greatest strengths is the "deracinated" attitude of its people—the enormous flexibility they show in taking diverging, even conflicting, concepts from abroad and using them out of context in a creative mix-and-match approach. Whatever the observation, if it helps us reexamine our conventional wisdom and compare our way of doing things, it is useful.

In the long run, however, the most useful application of the Japanese model may be as a "benchmark" or "yardstick." Statistics showing the U.S. with "x" times more lawyers than Japan may not mean Japan is better off, but it does suggest that in a modern society there are ways to resolve conflicts other than litigation. If our executives are far better paid than their Japanese counterparts, or if the gap between executive and worker compensation in America is far greater than in Japan, we need not conclude that we should adopt the Japanese system. But such figures may tell us why we have poor worker morale. Similarly, statistics showing that Japan has a lower infant mortality rate than ours, a higher literacy rate, and a lower defect rate in its cars, give us something to measure ourselves against and an incentive to do better. The actual means that we select to improve ourselves is irrelevant; what works best may not even come from Japan. But just by showing us there is another and sometimes better way, Japan performs an important service.

What Is the Japanese "Miracle"?

Lest we lose sight of the most important lesson, Japan is not a world model today because it has interesting aesthetics, crafts, religions, management techniques, or technologies. Plenty of other nations and cultures have those. Japan is a model because, starting from a humble position in 1945, it has amassed so much wealth and power in such a short time, without resorting to military might and without possessing vast natural resources. This, in essence, is the "Japanese miracle."

How did Japan do this? All the sociological mumbo-jumbo written about Japan aside, the macro-answer is actually quite simple. Japan acquired its wealth by importing raw materials, by manufacturing goods with increasingly more value added, and by exporting these goods on the world market. To do this it had to continually and incrementally refine the manufacturing process and its technology. Nearly every other area in which the Japanese method is held up as a modern model, whether it is quality control or business management or finance, is a subset of this single overriding reality. But to understand why Japan took the approach it did requires some background information.

Respect for Technology

When Commodore Matthew Perry arrived to force Japan out of its isolation in 1853, Japan had a highly developed social system but a level of technology stuck in the Middle Ages. It had some simple spinning wheels, a few Archimedean screw pumps for irrigating fields, some wheeled carts, and a few wooden mechanisms. But there were no telegraphs, steam trains, steamships, stagecoaches, and virtually no screws to hold things together. Large ships that could navigate open seas were banned, transportation on land was largely on foot, the few guns around were mostly pre-flintlock-stage matchlocks, and the main weapon was the sword.[23] Japan capitulated to Perry's demands for one reason, and it was not because America had an intrinsically superior civilization: it was because America had superior technology and superior firepower.

After 1853, under the slogan *fukoku kyohei*, or "Rich nation, strong military," Japan raced to import technology and industrialize, to catch up to the West and surpass it if possible. Its motivation was to avoid the fate of other Asian nations that had been colonized, and to preserve Japan's political sovereignty. The consensus on the need to do this was created by the overwhelming technological advantage that Perry had demonstrated.

The first indication of how successful Japan was at this strategy came fifty years later when its forces, using modern weapons and modern ships, trounced those of the Russian Empire. But then, leading up to World War II, Japan made a fatal mistake. Its leaders decided that any remaining technological handicap relative to the Western powers could be compensated for by superior "spirit," Japan's traditional (and still-thriving) anti-rational belief in the power of mind over matter.

In World War II, the Japanese military was not defeated so much by American moral superiority or bravery as by American mass-production technology—by the thousands upon thousands of ships and tanks and planes that American factories were able to churn out. The result was a bloody lesson pounded into the head of every person in Japan: science and technology, especially manufacturing technology, were a source of power and strength. Even Emperor Hirohito, in a letter to the crown prince after the war, admitted that Japan had lost because "our armed forces put too much emphasis on the spiritual side and forgot science."[24]

The lesson was capped by the atom bomb. In the United States, the bomb simultaneously led to an intoxication with the power of technology in warfare and great hand-wringing and self-reflection over its use—our use of the bomb, in fact, is responsible for much of the modern-day skepticism we have about science and technology. In Japan—the victim—the bomb had the opposite effect. It confirmed the futility of relying on military power alone, and it confirmed the need for superior science and technology.

After World War II, technology—especially manufacturing technology—became Japan's means of survival. With few natural resources, a constitutional ban on the use of military force to achieve national goals, and a desperate need to feed a population exploding with repatriated soldiers and colonists from throughout the former empire, there was only one route to take. That was to make goods for sale on the world market and to use the money earned for food and raw materials.

At the same time, America occupied, controlled, and fed defeated Japan. Anxious not to have it become a permanent financial burden or fall victim to communist ideology, it helped reform Japan's economy and industrial system and threw its own markets open to Japan's goods. As recently declassified documents show, the U.S. government encouraged American industry to use Japanese products (even though they did not meet existing quality standards) and it encouraged Japan to limit its imports.[25] To avoid creating a military competitor, it undertook Japan's defense. The result was a clarity of purpose rare in the history of nations—Japan would begin manufacturing goods of increasing sophistication, and export them.

In the future, Japan's economy may fall apart and its society may sink into decadence and disrepair. But that will not negate the fundamental truth of how it became a global model in the late twentieth century. Japan's emergence as a financial giant, its purchase of American film studios and property, and its increased global prominence in modern arts—all are a result of wealth earned from manufacturing increasingly sophisticated goods and selling them abroad, primarily to American consumers.

For generations of Americans who have spent a considerable amount of their national wealth on electronic gizmos and autos made in Japan, the challenge is figuring out how to earn some of that money back. And in this context, too, Japan has some very important lessons to teach us.

National Strategy

During the 1988 U.S. presidential campaign, then Vice-President George Bush savaged his hapless opponent, Michael Dukakis, sneering and accusing him of advocating what he said smacked of European- or Swedish-style "socialism": having a national industrial policy. This use of the ultimate weapon in twentieth-century American political discourse—of code words hinting of communist leanings—symbolized the fierce ideological battle that has long raged in America between those who espouse free-market ideologies and those who favor some sort of government guidance of industry.

Americans have long feared any sort of government intrusion into their lives or businesses, for good reason. Our nation was founded as an act of resistance to totalitarianism and outside interference, and throughout our history we have watched other nations try to control their economies and fail miserably. The centralized command economies of the Soviet Union and its client states and the nationalized economies of Latin American dictatorships have invariably led to a breakdown in the natural feedback system of the marketplace, to distortions in supply and demand, and to rampant inefficiencies, corruption, and stagnation. To distinguish ourselves ideologically from the makers of these economic disasters, we have held up the banner of the free market, and, especially under the Reagan-Bush years, of a laissez-faire ideology. In many circles, industrial policy has become a synonym for protectionism.

What this ideological focus has obscured, however, is that Japan and other East Asian nations following in its steps, plus several Western European nations (such as Sweden), have had considerable success with modified industrial policies, and that the U.S., partly due to its competition with the Soviet Union, has a de facto industrial policy of its own. To say we have no industrial policy today is like the atheist claiming he has no religion, while attending Atheist Society meetings every week. Our military, our space program, our agricultural and highway subsidies, even our protection of the auto industry have all been forms of industrial policy, promoted and directed by the federal government. The problem is they have often been extraordinarily inefficient policies, because they have been uncoordinated, and, worse, encouraged the wrong results. Starting in the mid-1970s, U.S. policies that encouraged consumption over production while continuing massive investment in a nonproductive military began running headfirst into the cumulative effect of Japanese policies that emphasized savings and investment and civilian production. The result was a trade deficit with Japan that ballooned to nearly $50 billion per year in 1993.

What is Japan's industrial policy? Essentially it is a set of policies that promote economic growth and further national interest by nurturing strategic industries, at the same time other industries are phased out when they are no longer competitive. These policies are formulated by elite government bureaucracies, the most famous of which is the former wartime Ministry of Munitions—today's Ministry of International Trade and Industry, or MITI—working in cooperation with industry.

The history of industrial policy in Japan is littered with failures, especially where protectionism has been involved. Japan's rice industry, for example, is hardly competitive with the rest of the world and in its pricing structure resembles a Soviet command-style economy. But in the area of manufacturing and high technology Japan has rung up some rather stellar successes, especially in the industries MITI has promoted, such as steel, mechatronics, lasers, semiconductors, and flat-panel displays. This has not required the government funding or the huge, heavy-handed bureaucracy one might expect, for, as a ratio of GNP, government spending in Japan has historically been much smaller than in the United States.[26] The most important role of the government has been as a coordinator. As Stanford University professor and MITI expert Daniel Okimoto notes, industrial policy for high technology in Japan "has served as the main instrument for consensus building, the vehicle for information exchange and public-private communication."[27]

The World of Value-Added Industries

A key tenet of free-trade ideology is that nations should specialize in what they do best; if they are best at producing potato chips, they should produce potato chips rather than computer chips. But in the real world, nearly all nations today want to industrialize and produce high-tech goods. This is not just for prestige. Some products have greater strategic value than others. Advanced computer chips contribute more to a nation's defense than potato chips, and manufacturing them can provide the know-how to start manufacturing in other areas with even more value added, such as cellular phones or high-definition television sets. And it is usually possible to charge more money for manufactured products that have greater value added—just as it is usually possible to charge more for potato chips than for raw potatoes. According to the concept known as "declining terms of trade," articulated by Raul Prebisch and Hans Singer in the 1950s, as incomes in nation rise, the demand for primary products grows slower than the demand for manufactured goods. Thus nations that export mainly raw materials or potatoes may face declining prices for their exports and have to pay more, relatively speaking, for their high-tech imports of Walkmans and TV sets.[28]

Japan thus determined early on that some industries would be more important than others, and it helped usher in new industries that stood a good chance of competing on the world market while easing out those that did not. These efforts to pick winners and losers did not always work as planned, and when overt promotion and protectionism—whether through direct government actions or government-encouraged intra-industry collusion—were employed, they enraged Japan's trading partners and threatened the free-trade system. But the strategy worked well enough so that in the aggregate Japan prospered.

Nothing better illustrates the difference between the U.S. approach and the Japanese approach than the robotics industry. The industrial robot was invented, developed, and first applied on a large scale in factories in the United States starting in the 1960s. As a complex, immature technology, however, the robot was extraordinarily difficult to use effectively. In the laissez-faire environment of the United States, when robots did not prove to be a quick fix for manufacturing problems, the industry withered and nearly died. But in Japan it flourished.

In Japan robots were early on perceived as a strategic industry worth developing, not just because robots can provide labor at less cost than humans, but because robots can also be more accurate, reliable, and clean. The government and its agencies encouraged robot manufacturers; it helped establish the JIRA, or Japan Industrial Robot Association, so robot manufacturers and users could work together to further their industry and share information; it initiated research programs in government laboratories that also involved private industry; it established technology transfer and training programs to help smaller manufacturers learn how to use robots; and it helped set up a system so that even smaller mom-and-pop type manufacturers could lease expensive robots and enjoy their benefits. All this created a synergistic effect that took manufacturers and users of industrial robots through a learning curve as they assembled the critical knowledge required to master these complex machines. In the end, Japanese makers of automobiles and electronics goods gained a substantial advantage over their American and European competitors in manufacturing cost and quality.

In the United States, because robotics technology was difficult and expensive, smaller manufacturers tended to shy away from it. When larger manufacturers using American-made industrial robots ran into quality and operational problems, they usually did one of two things: they reverted to the traditional drug of choice of American manufacturing, cheap human labor, or they turned to Japan for help.

In 1982 America's largest user of industrial robots, General Motors, formed a joint venture with one of Japan's largest and most aggressive robot manufacturers, Fanuc. GMF Robotics, as it was called, overnight became America's biggest robot manufacturer, but it relied almost exclusively on Japanese robot hardware. Because of the connection to GM and the huge economies of scale GMF enjoyed, this deal sounded the death knell for most domestic American robot manufacturers, who rapidly began dropping out of the competition.

By 1986 Japan had over 116,000 industrial robots at work in its factories, compared to only 25,000 in the United States. It also had around 300 manufacturers of robots, compared to around 50 in the U.S.[29] By 1992, according to the Robotic Industries Association of America, Japan was installing more robots each year than the *entire* installed U.S. robotics base.[30] Today American auto and electronics manufacturers make heavy use of robots, but most of these robots are made in Japan; in the American electronics industry many of the Japanese robots are actually at work in offshore factories, such as in Singapore. The deal between General Motors and Fanuc came unglued in 1992, with Fanuc buying GM's share and automatically becoming the largest robot supplier and "manufacturer" in America.

The robot industry is only a symbol of the larger computer-controlled machine tool industry and of the field Japanese call "mechatronics." With a little Japanese-style "administrative guidance," the United States could have encouraged the growth of such a strategic industry. This might have involved offering tax credits for use of robotics and establishment of a leasing system or technical assistance programs for smaller manufacturers, but it would not have required protectionism or cost very much money. A little more publicity over the propriety and implications of GM's joint venture with Fanuc might have helped too. Had the government adopted this strategy, more U.S. manufacturing might have stayed onshore, and U.S. manufacturers might have been better able to compete with Japan in quality and costs. And this, in turn, might have helped prevent the erosion of U.S. auto manufacturers' share, the loss of our consumer electronics industry, and the emergence of our huge trade deficit with Japan.

Product versus Process Technology

Japan's use of robots illustrates the importance of process, as opposed to product, technology. Product technology is the technology that goes into the design of the product, whether an automobile, VCR, Walkman, CD player, or airplane. It is the technology that is visible to the average person and also the easiest to imitate by "reverse engineering." The United States excels at product technology, and many of the products coming from Japan—even autofocus cameras and VCRs—are heavily dependent on licensed U.S. product technology. Process technology, however, is the technology that goes into the manufacturing of the product. It is the technology of robots and numerically controlled machine tools, "flexible manufacturing" systems, and quality control, and it is largely invisible to the average person. Process technology is the source of modern Japan's strength today, for it is what makes possible the mass production of increasingly diverse goods of increasingly higher quality at increasingly lower prices.

Despite having some of the highest labor costs in the world today, Japanese companies have made herculean efforts to keep manufacturing at home using advanced process technology. As the *Los Angeles Times* noted in 1992, Japanese firms were then manufacturing only 5 percent of their total production overseas, whereas the figure for American firms was 21 percent. Manufacturing accounted for 30 percent of GNP in Japan compared to less than 20 percent in the U.S.[31]

Why have Japanese manufacturers emphasized process technology and tried so hard to keep manufacturing at home? First, manufacturing by oneself has historically been a way of lessening dependence on imports (a form of "import substitution") and thus of preserving the nation's independence. More recently, it has been a way to provide the domestic workforce with jobs and to maintain a competitive advantage, for it offers a learning curve that will provide the strategic expertise and know-how to move to the next step of value-added manufacturing. Finally, the real profits and the jobs in the global trading system in recent years have come not so much from licensing—inventions or product technology—but from manufacturing high-volume items with increasingly greater value added.

For the United States, the lack of coordinated policies has meant not only that we have lost a great deal of manufacturing, but that we now rely much more heavily on Japanese and foreign components. This has created a vicious cycle. When our companies manufacture domestically and export anywhere other than Japan, it often contributes to a worsening of the trade deficit with Japan.

Our obsession with product versus process technology has also led to a serious delusion. Our media are filled with stories about how we are going to "leapfrog" Japan with this or that product technology, such as high-definition television, as if that will solve our trade problems. But no matter how wonderful our inventions or our products are, unless we develop the best means to manufacture them, they will be made overseas in Japan and other nations, where most of the jobs and the wealth will also be created.

Competition and Cooperation

There is plenty of evidence in America to suggest that, when left to the natural forces of the market, industries eventually gravitate toward a type of monopoly or oligarchy capitalism. Conventional wisdom also says that policies designed to help specific industries lead to "pork-barrel" politics and a drop in competitiveness.

An intriguing feature of Japan's industrial policy is that even among the targeted manufacturing industries there can be ferocious competition with relatively little consolidation. Japan's population is half that of the United States, but it has several times more automobile manufacturers, robot manufacturers, television manufacturers, computer memory manufacturers, photographic film manufacturers, and manufacturers in nearly every area in which Japan is competitive.

The key to this is the use of "administrative guidance" to lay out a middle ground between the absolute chaos of the free market on the one hand and the inefficiencies of centralized control on the other, to emphasize both competition and cooperation. Ezra F. Vogel claims one characteristic of Japanese society is an emphasis on "fair share," as opposed to an American emphasis on "fair play," and for many industries he is certainly right.[32] At the risk of overgeneralizing, rather than a "winner-takes-all" approach, at least in the domestic market, the major players appear to be willing to share the spoils.

Cooperation among companies in targeted industries is encouraged through government-sponsored research projects, industry associations, and consortiums. Many of the smaller-sized companies are already accustomed to a certain amount of cooperation with their immediate competitors because they belong to the larger industrial groupings that make up Japan's famous *keiretsu* systems. Then, after receiving some nurturing (and sometimes protection), the companies are quickly exposed to competition—both at home and in the world markets. Exports have historically been the ultimate training ground for Japanese manufacturers, forcing them to learn about foreign competitors, to adapt their products to foreign customers' tastes, and to improve their quality. As Sony's founder, Akio Morita, has noted, exporting forces an improvement in quality, not just to satisfy foreign customers but to reduce the high costs of servicing the products in distant places after the sales have taken place.[33]

What appear to be sinister Japanese actions in exports—of "dumping," or pricing below cost—can actually be accidental spin-offs of domestic Japanese competition. The Japanese call this *kajo kyoso* or "overcompetitiveness." Flat-panel displays used in laptop computers are an example. In late 1991, the U.S. Commerce Department slapped a tariff as high as 62.7 percent on Japanese-made displays, claiming they were being dumped in the U.S.[34] Japan's *Aera* magazine, in an article shortly thereafter titled "Charging Ahead with Red Ink—the LCD Wars," noted how, despite the absence of any real competition from abroad, Japanese manufacturers were engaged in an enormously costly pitched battle among themselves. They were all trying to perfect the extremely difficult flat-panel manufacturing technology in the hope of getting a piece of what was predicted to become a ¥2 trillion industry by the end of the century. One engineer quoted in the article said, "we're completely in the red, but we think of it as an investment for the twenty-first century, so we grin and bear it." Participation in this superheated competition, the article added, came partly from feeling the pressure of the Japanese mass media; for the manufacturers, it had become a matter of corporate face-saving.[35] In effect, the flat-panel displays were being dumped in Japan as well.

American businessmen have long complained of the unfair advantages their Japanese counterparts have had, from cheaper capital to lower labor costs. But many of these advantages have now disappeared, and American firms have begun emulating Japanese *keiretsu* groupings and forming consortiums. Japanese firms' biggest advantage may be that they have learned to cooperate with rivals where it benefits them and they have been exposed early on to fierce competition.

Investing in People

Japanese often describe their society as "wet," in contrast to America's, which is "dry," but they are not referring to rainfall or the consumption of alcohol. They mean that Japanese society puts enormous emphasis on human relationships—on feelings, moods, and duties—as opposed to America, which supposedly values contracts and legalistic, cut-and-dried relationships. This generalization is a bit wild (and slightly insulting), but it has an element of truth. Although in social services Japan greatly lags the United States, Japanese society does invest an extraordinary amount of time and money in bringing people together, building relationships, and achieving a consensus. According to some calculations, Japan spends four times more than the United States on corporate entertaining, but most of this really constitutes an investment in the relationships needed to do business and in *jinmyaku*—the chains of connections that make up Japanese society. Similarly, the long working hours of company employees serve to keep groups intact and to insure that a consensus is maintained. American business people working in Japan find the investment in human relationships exhausting but ultimately rewarding. It is one of the keys to cracking the Japanese market.

Japan's other investment in people is through education. Japan may appear to have few natural resources, but its educated population has proven to be its most important resource of all. Japan is not drowning in Nobel Prize winners (it has very few) and not everyone reads Tolstoy (publicity about high literacy rates aside, nearly 40 percent of all books and magazines published in Japan today are comic books). Japan does not even spend an inordinately large portion of its budget on schools. Japan has instead achieved a triumph of averages. Despite all its problems, Japan's basic educational system produces a work force that is literate, capable of basic math, and well socialized in that it knows how to work together and follow instructions. A Japanese high school education is probably the equivalent of an education at many colleges in the United States.

Given the dismal state of U.S. public schools, more and more American educators are studying the Japanese system. What they are finding is not that superior Japanese academic performance is related to Confucian heritage or genetics, or even to bigger budgets and smaller class sizes.

Rather, some simple, common-sense factors are at work. Nationally standardized curriculums and tests provide a type of quality control. Parental involvement in the child's education is also critical. American psychologists Harold W. Stevenson and James W. Stigler, who in 1992 wrote *The Learning Gap: Why Our Schools are Failing and What We Can Learn from Japanese and Chinese Education*, concluded from lengthy studies that it was more important to reward effort than innate ability. Noting that the American educational system tends to emphasize the latter, they describe how this exacerbates socioeconomic differences among the students. Japanese educational methods, they say, instead "give the great majority of citizens about the same educational start in life and tend toward social equality. Such social and economic benefits may in the long run prove to be important for both the health of a nation and its economic competitiveness."[36]

Japan is by no means an egalitarian society; it is obsessed with hierarchy. But starting people out equally and socializing them to work with each other is a lifelong theme. National health programs for pregnant women and infants help reduce infant mortality rates. In traditional arts and crafts, no matter how talented a pupil, he or she will spend long hours, even years, mimicking and perfecting a teacher's most basic moves before moving on to the next step. In public schools, almost all students take part in cleaning classrooms and hallways; in college dormitories they often start out cleaning toilets. It is also not unusual for the new, elite employees of major corporations to start out doing menial, manual labor. Their reward for this effort is respect, and the chance to advance to a higher level of learning.

This emphasis on an early, equal footing helps create a strong theme of equity in society, despite the existence of many other obvious inequalities. In large corporations, pay scales are determined not so much by ability as by seniority, so that people of the same age usually earn similar amounts. There is usually much less of a gap in base pay for Japanese workers and bosses than in America. The boss may receive enormous perks, but his relatively low base pay and his willingness to take some sort of token cut in pay during hard times help promote an appearance of solidarity with the workers (and in Japan appearances are very important). In society at large, at least until the boom of the 1980s, the tax system also reinforced a sense of equity. Surveys have consistently shown that over 90 percent of all Japanese have considered themselves members of the middle class and that, until recently at least, Japan has had one of the most even distributions of incomes in the world.[37]

Writing in their book on income distribution titled *How Rich Is Too Rich?*, Americans Herbert Inhaber and Sidney Carrol came to the following powerful conclusion about Japan: "The evidence is clear. The Japanese shook the world economically in large part because they avoided the tremendous sinks of wealth in Western countries. As they developed financially, the money was spread around more evenly than in their competitors' countries. Because more people shared in it, the ideas of the multitudes could go forward. This, we suggest, is the hidden benefit of Japan's relatively equitable income distribution."[38]

The message for Americans is not just that we pay an enormous price for our neglect of people, but that we can also do something about it. More emphasis on early education, better training of workers, better health care, a reformed tax code—all these things would help. In an increasingly diverse society where people seem to be more and more divided along rarely crossed class and racial lines, one wonders if even a short-term draft might help too—not a military or "service" draft, but a "socialization" draft, where people spend six months of their lives learning how to live and work with those of different backgrounds.

Increasing our investment in people and in social equity would surely pay off by creating a work force with higher average ability as well as solidarity and motivation.

Knowledge Acquisition

No matter how well people can read and write or work together, without knowledge they are like databases without data; that is, capable of very little. In Japan's case, the knowledge that has played such an important part in making it globally competitive has by and large come not from within, but from without. Soon after 1853, an aggressive campaign began to import the best of foreign knowledge. Foreign experts, many from the United States, were invited to teach in Japanese schools and universities. Young Japanese, denied information from abroad for two hundred and fifty years and practically exploding with curiosity, began streaming overseas, studying and observing.

This aggressive knowledge-acquisition movement continues today, even though Japan now has far less to learn from abroad. Japanese students still vie to attend U.S. universities and colleges. Groups of dark-suited businessmen armed with notebooks, cameras, and now camcorders still regularly head to the U.S. on "technical tours," visiting factories, laboratories, and industry counterparts. Such tours are organized by individual companies, industry associations, and government agencies connected with MITI, whose job it is to make sure Japan's industries have access to the best information possible, whatever its source. The businessman on his technical tour is alternately regarded as a joke or a "threat" by the Americans, but his purpose is simple—to acquire knowledge that can improve his own industry.

Acquiring knowledge from overseas has required the Japanese to do more than just go out and collect it. They have had to learn foreign languages, especially English. College graduates today have studied English for ten years and usually have difficulty with conversation, but if they are scientists or engineers they can read the literature of their field of expertise with the aid of dictionaries. What personal language skills cannot cover, translation supplements.

Sit in a modern Japanese house or office and just look around. Virtually *everything*—the doors, the walls, the windows, the stereo equipment, the elevators, the carpets, the lightbulbs, and even the bolts and screws and glue that hold them all together—is the product of imported knowledge, of technology introduced with the help of translation over the last one hundred and fifty years. One could just about say this of Japan's entire physical infrastructure.

Today, one of the greatest imbalances between Japan and the United States is not in the trade of automobiles or television sets, but in the flow of information. Far more information flows into Japan than out of it. This is not because Japanese people are deliberately hiding anything; unlike the United States, with its huge "black box" of classified military information, information on technology in Japan is surprisingly available, because most of it is commercial.

The true cause of the imbalance in the information flow is mainly apathy and lack of interest on the part of the United States. In 1991, the United States sent only 980 full-time students to Japan, compared to 48,000 Japanese who attended U.S. universities and colleges on student visas and 42,000 who took part in special-education programs of less than three months.[39] Two years later there were at least 25 Japanese researchers in the United States for every single U.S. researcher in Japan.[40] In 1990, only 82 Japanese books were translated and published in the United States, compared with more than 3,000 English titles that were translated into Japanese.[41] Although the number of Americans studying Japanese has soared in the last few years, the number of those capable of using the language on a professional level remains minuscule. Hard figures are difficult to come by, but there are probably only a few hundred professional translators of written technical Japanese in the entire United States, and perhaps only a dozen or so American-born interpreters capable of handling conference work.

Making things worse, many American businessmen and scientists still believe they can passively let Japanese information flow to them. They are willing to wait until Japanese people translate (at high cost) what they think foreigners should know, rather than the other way around. Or they are willing to let the Japanese side bring the interpreters to discussions, ignoring the fact that the interpreter will always provide better service to the person footing the bill. This arrogance probably comes from our false sense of security as a military superpower, and our belief that foreign nations have little to teach us (the NIH, or "Not Invented Here," syndrome). But this thinking is extremely naive. With more and more original research being done in Japan in micromachines, artificial intelligence, robotics, ceramics, and fiber optics, and with Japanese corporations now rich enough to buy entire overseas research labs, those who cling to the outdated notion that Japanese are uncreative copycats do so at their own risk.

Learning a little Japanese could improve the information imbalance. The insurmountability of the Japanese language is a myth maintained by those who want to encourage notions of Japanese racial and linguistic uniqueness or who have simply found Japanese harder to learn than European languages. True fluency in Japanese takes years of study, but true fluency is rarely required. For a scientist, learning how to read may be more important than speaking. For a businessman, learning the cultural aspects of business and a few phrases, and then learning how to effectively use an oral interpreter or written translator, may be enough. Any effort is usually well rewarded.

Ultimately, Americans need more Japanese information because we have a $50 billion trade deficit with Japan, and our future prosperity rests at least in part on our ability to keep up with Japanese technology and to design and create products that Japanese consumers want to buy. A partial solution is to do what Japan has long been doing—encourage more language skills and exchanges of students and researchers, learn to use translation and interpretation properly, send teams of Americans from all types of industries to Japan, and hire some real Japanese expertise. Some of these measures have already begun—as symbolized by the U.S.-Japan Manufacturing Technology Fellowship Program or the Japan Technology

Program in the Department of Commerce, and by Japan-related programs at MIT and the University of Wisconsin—but they are not enough.

Familiarizing ourselves with our competitor will bring other benefits. Dennis Bushness, a respected NASA scientist, has noted that two-thirds of scientific information is now generated outside the U.S. and that most U.S. scientists and engineers are ignoring it.[42] Learning to learn from Japan will help us learn how to learn from other nations, too.

Fluency in Japanese might also take some of the surprises out of U.S.-Japan political relations. Shintaro Ishihara's 1989 book, *The Japan That Can Say No*, made sensitive Americans howl with wounded pride over what were fairly mild criticisms, but if these same Americans had been more familiar with Japanese thinking unfiltered by the English-language media they would hardly have been shocked. Prime Minister Kiichi Miyazawa's remarks in 1992 that were widely interpreted as a put-down of American workers would probably never have become an issue if the foreign reporters covering him had had a better knowledge of Japanese and realized he was really criticizing Japan. Better knowledge of Japan may not make Americans like Japanese people more, but it might help defuse the gross stereotypes some Americans cling to; that Japanese women are all downtrodden, that the men are all robotlike workers or racists, and—perhaps worst of all—that Japanese people have no sense of humor.

Long-Term Perspective

It has become a cliche to say that Japanese people have a "long-term perspective," as if this were some exclusive, Asian trait. American long-term thinking has resulted in vast national parks, a trip to the moon, and victory in a fifty-year-long cold war with communism. So where does this generalization about Japan come from?

For the past decade or so, Japan has seemed remarkably forward-looking. Japan's media have been filled with references to the "twenty-first century" as if it were about to dawn tomorrow and usher in a glorious new age of wealth and friendly technologies (presumably led by Japan). To Americans raised during the cold war, who feared their future would terminate in a thermonuclear meltdown, such optimism about the future may seem naive. But who can blame the Japanese for their hopefulness? According to a 1993 survey in the *Economist*, per-capita real income in Japan rose 7.7 percent per year between 1950 and 1990, from $1,230 (in 1990 prices) to $23,970. In the United States in the same period, income grew only 1.9 percent per year and is now surpassed by Japan.[43]

A more important manifestation of "long-term perspective" is the Japanese company executive who plans further ahead and is less fixated on the need to turn a quick profit than his American counterpart. There is nothing "cultural" about this either. Japanese executives in publicly held firms usually report to their shareholders only every half year or year, and may occasionally even withhold dividends. American executives normally have to report to their shareholders four times a year, so they can hardly afford to look very far into the future. U.S. economist Lester Thurow strongly advocates changing the American system. Merely switching to a twice-a-year or once-a-year reporting system, he contends, would greatly lengthen managers' horizons.[44]

The pursuit of large-scale national projects in which both government and industry cooperate is another reflection of Japan's reflection of Japan's long-term perspective. Many such projects—whether in artificial intelligence, robotics, or high-definition television—are initiated with absurdly lofty goals. And then, when the projects fail to reach these goals, they are often belittled in the United States. Japan's Fifth Generation Project, designed in 1981 to develop artificial intelligence systems that could mimic human thinking, at first generated panic among American scientists, who now call it a flop. But such a project provides extraordinary learning opportunities above and beyond its stated goal—just as the Apollo project to put a man on the moon had no immediate application but led to valuable commercial spin-offs like Teflon cookware. Spin-offs from

Japan's Fifth Generation Project may already have found application in Japanese word-processor technology, thus helping to bring a largely handwriting, scribe-based society into the computer age in less than twenty years, practically leapfrogging the entire typewriter stage of civilization that most of the rest of the world went through. Large-scale national projects help mobilize business, government, and academic resources in pursuit of a single long-term goal at relatively low cost, and they provide a national learning experience.

The biggest symbol of Japan's long-term perspective is its high savings rate, because it gives Japan a huge competitive advantage, permitting, among other things, heavy investment in modern manufacturing technology. Like everything else in Japan, however, the savings rate is not driven by culture alone—there are powerful, rational incentives to save. The social security system in Japan, for example, is less developed than in most other advanced industrialized nations; people *have* to save for their own retirement. Also credit cards and easy loans were hard to obtain until recently, which put a damper on consumption (when cards did become widely available, an epidemic of *kaado hasan*, or "credit card bankruptcies," occurred). And the Ministry of Posts and Telecommunications encourages savings at its 24,000 local post offices, often at interest rates higher than most private banks can offer. Until a few years ago, interest on savings of up to ¥8 million (nearly $80,000 at 1993 rates) was tax-free, and a legal loophole allowed people to routinely open multiple accounts under names of other family members—at one point there were three accounts for every single person in Japan.[45] By 1992 the Japanese government had amassed a mind-boggling fund of $1.29 trillion that it could use for investment purposes.[46]

Human behavior is not as cultural as we think. A long-term perspective could be fostered in the United States by the simple means of changing government policy.

Humanist Ideals

The jaws of American businessmen and women often sag in astonishment over the language used in Japanese business speeches and negotiations. It sounds, at times, like New Age rhetoric, filled with long-winded references to mutual trust and understanding, human happiness, and world peace, while containing scarcely any mention of the real life-blood of business—money. And the same language is used by officials during terribly serious government negotiations over trade and politics. After long-winded and lofty, seemingly hopelessly out-of-touch pronouncements, one wonders, When are they going to get to the point? Yet this language embodies what may be one of modern Japan's greatest strengths—a people-oriented ideology.

In America today ideology is often negatively associated with totalitarian governments, and especially with international communism, which suffocated in its own dogma. Yet all nations (including the United States) and all corporations operate with some sort of ideology, even if it is not clearly defined. The soft, fuzzy language in which Japanese businessmen and government officials envelop themselves does not mean they are not cut-throat negotiators, or that they are less Machiavellian than their American counterparts; they may, in fact, be more so. But an ideology with the goal of worker welfare, human happiness, and global peace—as opposed to an ideology of the primacy of profits—can be a powerful influence on work-force morale and customer preferences. It becomes what the Japanese might call (with only a trace of cynicism) *tatemae*, or a statement of "intent."

The way technology diffuses through Japanese society illustrates this. Japan is extraordinarily receptive to new technologies. Technology came to Japan late, so the Japanese people were spared much of the trauma of the industrial revolution and of having to act as guinea pigs for emerging technologies. In the postwar period Japan's defense has largely been handled by the United States. Japanese technology, therefore, has also been relatively free from the stigma of association with the military and killing—a stigma particularly strong in the United States among Vietnam-era Americans, many of whom once viewed U.S. technology corporations as purveyors of death. And since so much of Japanese business has been civilian-oriented, Japanese companies have always had to think first of using technology to create products that will appeal (and sell) to humans.

Today, Japan's technology goals—whether for robotics, computers, artificial intelligence, or virtual reality—are formulated within the government and the corporations, but it is Japan's powerful media, with the help of huge advertising agencies like Dentsu and Hakuhodo, that end up making them palatable to the citizenry. Buzzwords related to the goal of the technology soon start appearing in commercials, on products, and even in toy stores. Manufacturers spend enormous amounts of time and money promoting the "image" of the technology as something warm and fuzzy, offering universal benefits. They front the public introductions of their products with innocent and attractive young females in uniforms, and they cloak themselves in "human" terms—the "Sociotech" of Mitsubishi, the "Humanication" of Hitachi, and the "Built for the Human Race" of Nissan. In no time at all, the average person in the street is mouthing "AI", "Fuzzy Logic," or "VR," and using products emblazoned with these words, often without having the slightest idea what they really mean. Sometimes the technology fads reach a dead end or disappear altogether, but if all goes well they create an extraordinary momentum for competition on all levels of society. There is a tremendous amount of money at stake here, and the battle over it is ferocious, but the prize is corporate and national pride, and consumer loyalty.

There is a moral here for Americans. We have been forced to play global policeman and to mix civilian and military technology. We (and the Europeans) bore many of the burdens of the industrial revolution. But at the same time we have also promoted an ideology that sometimes seems to imply everything in life can be quantified in terms of dollars and cents or formalized in legal contracts, or that human nature can always be explained in terms of economic self-interest. And sometimes we seem to have forgotten the importance of a larger goal. In introducing new technologies, in business, and even in international relations, a "soft," humanistic ideology can be a powerful tool.

* * * * *

Japan's economic success derives from a unique set of historical and cultural circumstances. In attempting to learn from Japan's success, we have to be able to distinguish between myth and reality, to understand why Japan does better or worse in some areas than we do without getting bogged down in cultural generalizations. Ultimately, the methods we select to improve our own society, and the means by which we implement these methods, will have to be tailored to the conditions and the age in which we live. And they will probably have to be American and original.

There is no guarantee that Japan's success will continue. Japan's advantages of being a late starter (of being able to learn from the mistakes of others and being able to license needed technology at low cost) and of having its defense needs largely shouldered by the United States, will probably end soon. Having single-mindedly pursued and now achieved its materialistic goal of "catching up with the West," Japan may now begin to flounder spiritually, and its much vaunted social consensus may begin to fray at the edges.

Nonetheless, we can say that Japan's success up until around 1990 was the result of making the right decisions at the right time and of cleverly marshaling its limited human and physical resources toward the larger goals: promoting economic growth and advancing Japan in the hierarchy of nations. The lesson from Japan is that economies are like fruit trees; if nurtured, watered, and carefully tended, they may bear better fruit.

Japan is a world model not just because it has become rich, but because of where it started and how it got to where it is now. After being devastated in World War II, Japan triumphantly demonstrated that it is not necessary to have extensive natural resources or a great military in order to amass power and wealth, that wealth can be acquired by working intelligently and peacefully, within the context of the free-trade system. Lest we forget, this is a relatively new notion in human history.

Just as important, by acquiring and mastering "Western" science and technology and using it to compete successfully with both America and Europe, Japan in effect "desegregated the bus." Modern science and technology was developed and monopolized by primarily Caucasian, Judeo-Christian, and European civilizations, and the extraordinary advantage it gave them helped give rise to myths of racial supremacy, to colonialism, and to the obliteration of indigenous cultures around the world. Japan has demonstrated, for once and for all, that race and religion are not prerequisites to the mastery of capitalism or science and technology. In the process, for other nations outside the European tradition, it has made itself a shining role model. For the United States, which has embarked upon a multiracial, multicultural social experiment at home, predicated on the ability of all peoples to learn and to master science and technology, Japan's success—rather than a threat—is a thrilling affirmation of the correctness of our approach.

FOUR

Mirror

*What an education the Orient is! How it opens a
man's eyes and mind about his own country, about
conventionalisms of a hundred sorts. . . .*

Lafcadio Hearn,
in a letter to a friend, May 12, 1893

*I*n 1883, before becoming a famous astronomer and a propagandist for the idea of intelligent life on Mars, Percival Lowell visited Japan. In the book he later wrote, *The Soul of the Far East*, he reassured his fellow Americans that, no, Japanese people do not really stand upside down because they live on the other side of the earth, but that everything else about them is nonetheless quite topsy-turvy. Japanese speak, read, and write backward, he said, and this is "but the *abc* of their contrariety." Like the writer Lafcadio Hearn, who found Japan "a queer thrill impossible to describe,"[1] Lowell delighted in observing such things as the way Japanese turned struck matches away from instead of toward themselves, pulled saws instead of pushing, and stood wet umbrellas on their handles instead of their heads to dry. He found the Japanese so simultaneously like and unlike Occidentals that he said, "we seem, as we gaze at them, to be viewing our own humanity in some mirth-provoking mirror of the mind,—a mirror that shows us our own familiar thoughts, but all turned wrong side out."[2]

Today Japan is so similar to America that the early American adventurers would surely be disappointed. But Japanese books still start at the "back," the basic word order of the language is still virtually the opposite that of English, people drive (as in England) on the "wrong side of the road," and at times people still sound like they're saying "yes" when they mean "no." And on a more abstract level, too—on the level of cultural generalizations—Japan and America are often said to be one hundred and eighty degrees apart. Japanese society is "group-oriented" while America's is "individual-oriented." Japanese social organization is "vertical" while America's is "horizontal," and on and on. Most of these generalizations are only differences in emphasis, but there are enough of them to keep Americans busy writing about Japan for centuries. And probably half the books about Japan are really books about America. For all its similarities to America, Japan is still the perfect mirror-image metaphor for America and the perfect place for us to form a new frame of reference.

Japan's Successes Reflect America's Successes

One of the great ironies of Americans using Japan as a model today is that so many of the things being emulated actually have their roots in the United States.

For years after World War II, Japanese engineers were notorious for their ability to "copy" others' products down to the most minute details. Older American engineers still tell stories, perhaps apocryphal, of analyzing an advanced product from a Japanese competitor and finding it identical to theirs down to the flaws in the original design. Today Japanese are rarely accused of being copycats, and are more likely to be admired, if not for their pure creativity, at least for their ability to take ideas from the United States—ideas that Americans have often neglected—and then develop them in an original fashion.

Quality control, a hallmark of Japanese manufacturing, is one of the best-known examples. Incorporating and refining American quality-control techniques enabled Japan to break out of the manufacturing ghetto it was in after the war, when being a low-cost supplier of low-quality goods made "Made in Japan" a joke rather than a badge of pride. The gurus of this movement were American management consultants like W. Edwards Deming and J. M. Juran, who were ignored in their homeland even as they were turned into the demigods of manufacturing in Japan. Both men have received Japan's Order of the Sacred Treasure and have prestigious national quality awards named after them. The Baldridge Award in the U.S., created at the end of the 1980s, was a response to Japan's highly successful "Deming Prize."[3]

Industrial robotics, which flourished in Japan, was also imported from the United States, but most people at least know the technology originated in America. JIT or "Just-In-Time" manufacturing, which stresses eliminating waste from the manufacturing process and, in particular, keeping inventory to a minimum, is believed by many Americans to have come from Japan, when in fact it originated in the 1920s in the United States with the Ford Motor Company.[4] Even the *kaizen* philosophy of continuous improvement, which American manufacturers are today energetically adopting, is rooted in America. Many of its techniques come from the company TWI (Training Within Industries) and the U.S. Air Force.[5]

Despite their occasional claim that they have little left to learn from the United States, Japanese businessmen are still incorporating American management fashions. In 1992 one of the most popular buzzwords in Japanese industry was "CS," an acronym for "Customer Satisfaction," and Japanese blue-chip companies were busy forming CS action groups. As *Aera* magazine explained it, CS was a philosophy that had originated in the United States in the 1980s "when American corporations introduced Japanese TQC concepts in order to compete with the 'Made in Japan' products then taking over the market."[6] But of course TQC, an acronym for "Total Quality Control" (or "Commitment"), was itself really an outgrowth of the postwar research of Americans like Deming.

Ideas ignored in the United States frequently become "movements" in Japan. "Fuzzy logic" is a field of mathematics that, compared to binary processing, allows a more humanlike way of dealing with approximate data to find precise solutions. Pioneered by Lotfi A. Zadeh, a professor at the University of California, Berkeley, it has had slow acceptance in the United States. Yet in Japan it now helps control trains, automobiles, washing machines, and auto-focus camcorders. In 1991 Japan reportedly controlled nearly 80 percent of what was estimated to be a multibillion dollar world market for the technology. Influenced by Japan's successes, more and more American manufacturers are reinvestigating fuzzy logic and applying it to their problems.[7]

"Cold fusion," which holds out the promise of infinite, cheap, nonpolluting power, may prove to be a similar story. University of Utah scientists B. Stanley Pons and Martin Fleischmann originally "discovered" this dramatic new technology in 1989, but they were widely derided and mocked in the United States when their research results could not be replicated by others. A few years later, Japan had formed a government-industry consortium to investigate cold fusion. Pons and Fleischmann were continuing their work in France at a Toyota-financed laboratory.[8]   .

Sometimes even American popular culture does better in Japan than at home. Japan has its own long tradition of cartooning, but the format of Japanese comic books is basically a twentieth-century import from the United States. After briefly flowering in America, comic books were attacked in the 1950s by a coalition of conservative forces claiming comics were a corrupting influence on youth. Under pressure, publishers instituted a draconian system of self-censorship, and artists confined themselves to safe and sanitized tales of morally correct superheroes. Circulations plummeted, publisher bankruptcies soared, and comics were stigmatized as a medium for juveniles. They have never quite recovered. But in Japan, American-style comics have had spectacular success. They are read today by nearly all sectors of the population. Their visual stories in serialized form go on for thousands of pages and deal with themes ranging from romance to picking stocks and bonds. Comics in Japan are a full-fledged medium of narrative entertainment on a par with novels, films, and television.

Whether robots, fuzzy logic, or comic books, Japan's ability to pick up fumbled American ideas and run with them represents more than lost American opportunities. It suggests that Americans may not always realize what's good about America. Japanese—perhaps because they can view things at a distance, unshackled by U.S. preconceptions—often have a better idea of our real strengths than we do ourselves.

Democratic Ideals

A surprising number of the most lauded characteristics of postwar Japanese society—often cited as reasons for Japan's economic success—in fact have their roots in America and were imported during the Occupation. These include the general demilitarization, or commercial orientation, of Japan's economy; the humanization and democratization of the work force; equality in education; land reform; and the makings of a relatively classless society.

Between 1945 and 1952, the United States military controlled Japan and under the direction of General Douglas MacArthur carried out sweeping reforms. Unlike Germany—where the United States had to share spheres of influence with the French and British and the Soviets, and where the country was physically partitioned into Communist and non-Communist halves—in Japan the United States had a largely free hand. Japan became a test tube for American social reformers, many of whom were heavily influenced by the policies of Roosevelt's New Deal. Flush with the success of military victory over two powerful enemies, and economic victory over the Great Depression, they represented the U.S. at its idealistic peak.

MacArthur's orders from the Joint Chiefs of Staff were to "democratize" Japan. This involved not only demilitarizing Japan and instituting government, labor, and educational reforms, but encouraging and showing favor "to policies which permit a wide distribution of income and ownership of the means of production and trade."[9]

As Kazuo Kawai has noted in *Japan's American Interlude*, neither the Japanese nor the Americans in charge of carrying out the reforms always had a good idea of what democracy really was, and often "tended to equate [it] uncritically with the American way of life, which all too often carried connotations of central heating, big autos, and PX privileges."[10] But the Occupation reforms nonetheless strengthened Japan. Demilitarization freed up its resources and its people for commercial purposes. Encouraging exports and competition on the world market helped integrate Japan more tightly into the family of nations than ever before, thus setting it on its present trade-oriented course. Political and educational reforms unleashed the intellectual energies of the Japanese people and allowed greater numbers of common people to take an active role in planning and managing national life.

The American-authored constitution gave women the right to vote

for the first time; in several respects it was more liberal than even the Constitution of the United States. In addition to the right to "life, liberty, and
the pursuit of happiness," the Japanese constitution guaranteed academic
freedom, freedom from censorship, freedom from "discrimination in political, economic or social relations because of race, creed, sex, social status
or family origin," "the right to maintain the minimum standards of
wholesome and cultured living," and the right of all people "to receive an
equal education correspondent to their ability, as provided for by law." To
make sure no one took too much advantage of the new freedoms, the constitution also gave all people "the right and obligation to work." [11]

Land reforms and other social policies helped establish what, at least
until the go-go years of the 1980s, has been another hallmark of Japanese
society—a strong sense of social equity and an overwhelming middle-
class consciousness. As Kawai notes, the American occupiers completely
prohibited absentee landlordism and transferred over five million acres of
land to former tenants, making them all little capitalists with a stake in
the nation. An attempt to break up Japan's giant prewar conglomerates, or
zaibatsu, although never completed, nonetheless helped spread the existing wealth around and enabled smaller firms, like postwar mavericks
Sony and Honda, to later flourish. To help Japan get back on its economic
feet, MacArthur and his men also helped institute the "Dodge Plan."
Named for Detroit banker and later Director of the Budget of the United
States Joseph M. Dodge, it made sure that American aid was channeled
almost entirely into basic production instead of consumption and that the
Japanese would tax themselves heavily enough to expand their invest-
ments. [12]

As General MacArthur noted in the early days of the Occupation,
"you cannot teach democracy to a hungry people." A smoothly functioning democracy required a certain level of economic well-being, and in the
long run it required a modicum of social equity. It still does. In the United
States today, chronic poverty is growing, 37 percent of the nation's wealth
is now said to be concentrated in 1 percent of the nation's families, the

compensation of top chief executive officers is said to have risen from 35 times that of an average employee's pay in 1970 to 120 times in 1990, and the nation's internal and external balance of payments is completely out of whack.[13] The Occupation reformers would probably prescribe the same medicine for our ills today that they did for Japan nearly a half-century ago.

Japan's Problems Reflect America's Problems

American Joseph Engelberger, the "father of the industrial robot," likes to say that he is not too worried about Japan because the Japanese "are adopting our bad qualities as fast as they are our good qualities."[14] It is easy to overlook the fact that Japan experiences many of the same problems our society does and that Japanese people tend to worry about the same things we do, although with a five- or ten-year time lag.

Older generations of Japanese—like people everywhere—deride younger generations, and their complaints are magnified by the sheer enormity of change their society has gone through. The generation that matured in the early postwar years lived in a world of personal deprivation, and the personal sacrifices they made for their companies, families, and nation are in large part responsible for Japan's postwar economic "miracle." Younger generations—especially those born after 1965—have matured in affluence and the same intellectual environment as their American counterparts. They are strikingly different from their elders in appearance, habits, and values. Labeled the *shinjinrui*, or "New Humans," by the media, they are relentlessly criticized for marching to a different drummer, for being soft, effete, self-centered, and more inclined to spend time with friends, family, and hobbies than working overtime at the company.

As older Japanese throw their hands up in despair over the New Humans, many of Japan's competitors have pinned their hopes on them, believing they will finally take the edge off Japan's competitiveness and even send it into gradual decline. Whether this will happen is debatable, but like their native-born American counterparts, younger generations of Japanese do tend to avoid work that falls into the "3D"—Dirty, Dangerous, and Dull—category. This, coupled with a chronic labor shortage in the late 1980s and a deliberate attempt by the Japanese government to "internationalize," means more and more manufacturers have begun to rely on inexpensive, illegal foreign labor for work that can't be automated, in the same way many American manufacturers rely on legal and illegal foreign immigrants.

Japan is still a long way from an American-style racial salad bowl, but for a nation that has long boasted of its homogeneity, it is becoming rather diversified. Iranians or Brazilian-Japanese now work in neighborhood factories, and Southeast Asians wash dishes in restaurants. In rural areas some Japanese farmers have taken Southeast Asian, Chinese, and even Russian brides because Japanese women shun marriage with them. These new residents of Japan have brought with them a wonderful diversity to a sometimes monotonously homogeneous society, but they have also introduced a familiar set of problems. There is increased friction between locals and newcomers, discrimination, and increases in petty crime caused by poverty (in 1993 public phone booths in Tokyo's Minato Ward contained warnings against vandalism in twelve languages, including English, Korean, Portuguese, Farsi, and German). And there are also fears that more foreigners will come. Like paranoid Americans, paranoid Japanese worry that their cushy country will be inundated by waves of economic and political refugees from poorer neighbors.

More and more young Japanese also mirror young Americans in the very American quality called "attitude." For years, tourists in Tokyo have enjoyed watching Japanese teenagers dressed up in U.S. styles preen and dance near Harajuku Station on the weekend, affecting a cool decadence. For all their efforts, such teenagers often seem hopelessly well behaved to Americans, but all things are relative. Compared to previous generations, they do have a different attitude. In 1993 Japanese writer Kizo Ogura observed the same thing from the perspective of Korea, which many Japanese say resembles the Japan of ten years or so ago. Writing about elite, Americanized young Koreans, or what is called the "Orange Tribe," he noted that compared with Japanese they still retain many Confucian values. When trying to seduce a young woman, he observed, a young Korean man would tell her he's "an honest and good person," whereas a Japanese young man "would strike a pose and tell her he used to be a delinquent."[15]

Japan's low crime rate is still the envy of the modern world, but Japanese youth are proving to be almost as susceptible to the corrupting influences of excess media, free time, easy money, and lack of goals as anyone else. Juvenile delinquency is on the rise, and 1992 police reports show that use of drugs, including cocaine, heroine, and amphetamines, while minuscule compared to that in the United States, is growing substantially among Japanese youth.[16] Like their Western counterparts two decades ago, more and more young Japanese adventurers and hippies have been visiting Indonesia and Thailand in quest of hallucinogenic "magic mushrooms" and getting into trouble. And they're not the only ones. In 1993 even the head of one of Japan's largest media companies was arrested for his use of marijuan and cocaine.[17]

Japanese women—in the past known for their subservience to men— now appear more willing than men to defy convention. Popular artist Shungiku Uchida has created several confessional comic books about her own life and the problems she had with drugs, delinquency, and sex in high school. In 1992, along with appearing nude in a music video and going public with stories of being molested as a child, she announced she was pregnant with the child of a married male friend and proceeded to proudly give birth to a baby boy named Alpha—while continuing her relationship with her live-in boyfriend. She made news in Japan, but no more than a celebrity in America would.[18]

The list of changes in Japanese society, and of "American-style" problems goes on and on. The Japanese establishment and media worry about exactly the same things the American establishment worries about, including competition and dumping from low-wage countries, an overemphasis on consumption, a decline in the rate of savings, a waning work ethic, AIDS, and obesity, increased sexual promiscuity, and decreased literacy among young people. To see modern America today, we need look no further than Japan.

America through Japanese Eyes

As the crammed shelves in every bookstore in Japan testify, Japanese people have an abiding obsession with America. They love to read things written by Americans that criticize them, partly out of a narcissistic curiosity, and partly out of a desire to understand themselves better. Unfortunately, very little that Japanese have written on America—either complimentary or critical—has been published in English. This is a pity, for it can teach us much, not only about Japan, but ourselves.

Japanese attitudes toward the United States vary about as much as American attitudes toward Japan. Generational differences play a large part, because those born before the war experienced heavy anti-American propaganda, while those born after did not. But one's wartime experience—or lack of it—is by no means the only criterion for liking or disliking America.

Many Japanese people do like America, but because America's influence has been so overwhelming in their lives the relationship is probably best described as love-hate. As Japanese lawyer Naoyuki Agawa, an avowed fan of America born during the Occupation, wrote in a 1993 book titled *Amerika ga kirai desuka* [Do You Dislike America?], "Japanese feelings about America have always been complex. Admiration has been mixed with jealousy, respect has contained scorn. And while worrying out loud about America's decline, there has also been a tendency to secretly rejoice in it."[19] Ruiko Yoshida—a photojournalist formerly married to an American—lived in the U.S. for years and then made a conscious decision to return to Japan. In 1986 she wrote *Yoshida Ruiko no Amerika* [Ruiko Yoshida's America] and emblazoned its cover with the English words "Hate but Love." She says she hates the United States for its hysterical anticommunism, its superpower obsession with being number one, its slaughter of the Indians and enslavement of the Africans, and its arrogant disregard of the suffering of people in smaller, poorer countries during its military ventures. But, she says, she has a deep, continuing love affair with the American people and for America's emphasis on individual freedoms.[20]

Overt criticism of the United States falls into distinct categories. Until recently, Marxist thought had such a strong influence on the labor movement and the intellectual community that many criticisms ran predictably parallel to Japanese leftist criticisms of the Japanese system itself. These included criticisms of the excesses of capitalism, the exploitation of workers, tendencies toward colonialism and imperialism, and so on. Because these criticisms are so unsurprising, they are not as useful as some of other things Japanese say about us.

In recent years, as Japan's strength and self-confidence have grown and America's problems have been given more and more exposure, criticism of America has come from an increasingly broader spectrum of Japanese society. The most visible criticisms, again, are familiar to us, for they reflect the same sentiments that many Americans have about their own society—that the crime rate is too high, that people are not being educated properly or working hard enough, that not enough attention is going into quality control and manufacturing. These are the sort of arguments presented by Akio Morita and Shintaro Ishihara in their book *The Japan That Can Say No* and the sort of arguments American politicians like to adopt for campaign speeches.

The least-heard criticisms of America (and the most interesting) are more subjective and emotional. These are not the sort of complaints one hears from Japanese who work with Americans, that we talk too loud, talk too much, or eat too much for our own good. They are more sweeping and serious. They are not expressed directly but couched in oblique references to some larger context, and they are often linked to Japanese nationalism and tinged with paranoia. They are frequently indicative of subcurrents of thought in the general population.

In a land where comics have more influence than books, Kaiji Kawaguchi's best-selling series *Chinmoku no Kantai* [Silent Service] gives a hint of some rarely voiced popular emotions. A fantastical tale that began serialization in 1989 and lasted for thousands of pages, the comic is about a renegade Japanese nuclear submarine that humiliates the Soviet and United States navies with its superior tactics and technology. The submarine's goal is world peace and nuclear disarmament and the establishment of a transnational military force under the auspices of the United Nations. A major subtheme is Japanese irritation over U.S. world hegemony and its control over Japan, coupled with a strong sense of "historical inevitability" that Japan is destined to lead the world with its superior technology and moral force. Although purely entertainment, *Silent Service* became a sensation and stimulated debate on Japan's "Peace" constitution and Japan's role in the world. It was mentioned in Japan's parliament, granted awards, and loudly proclaimed by its publisher in large ads in major newspapers to have "awakened Japan from its slumber." Although Kawaguchi certainly never intended it, his comic sold especially well among younger members of the Self-Defense Forces and the right wing, some of whom reportedly took to calling him a new "Yukio Mishima"—a reference to the Nobel Prize–winning novelist who disemboweled himself after a failed attempt to engineer a right-wing coup d'état in 1970.[21]

Ryuichi Nagao: The End of the American Century

A more highbrow criticism of the United States appeared in 1991 in *Chuokoron*, an influential monthly dedicated to foreign affairs. Written by Professor Ryuichi Nagao of the elite Tokyo University at a time when U.S.-Japan relations were particularly rocky (during the unpopular Gulf War but before the sobering economic recession of 1992-94), it was titled "The Curtain Is about to Come Down on 'The American Century.'" Nagao's thesis is that while the twentieth century was indeed America's, the Protestant-style enterprising spirit that supported U.S. imperialism during this period is in decay and on the verge of disintegration, and the environmental problems caused by it will plague the next century. No firebrand America-hater, Nagao's arguments are fairly well reasoned.

During the Occupation, Nagao says, General Douglas MacArthur carried out an "Americanization" plan which—aside from failing to Christianize Japan—worked beyond anyone's expectations in terms of system reforms. The legal system, the *zaibatsu*-controlled economy, and even the political system were democratized. But in its economic development and in the vigor of its capitalism, Nagao says, pantheistic Japan went on to surpass the U.S. Why? Present-day U.S. methods of management are based on the Frederick Taylor and Henry Ford systems of scientific management in mass production, and are supported by a Pavlovian or Skinnerian view that most human behavior is conditioned and reflexive—that man is not "homo sapiens" so much as "homo economicus" and motivated only by short-term self-interest. This American belief in the ability to quantify all human behavior, Nagao says, is one of the root problems now confronting both U.S. businesses and educational systems.

Meanwhile, Japan, although it adopted the superficial form of U.S. culture in its corporations, in fact preserved the traditions of its old militarist culture—which demanded submersion of the individual ego into the group—by transforming the corporation into a sports-team style organization. In this new type of organization, the employees—not the shareholders or capitalists—reign supreme, and to them the company is a type of religion, a place to which they devote their lives and even sacrifice themselves in exchange for a sense of belonging, security, and identity. Compared to the Western- or Protestant-style religion of "individualism," this is a religion of "groupism" and the ultimate, perhaps unbeatable, form of capitalism.

The American spirit of capitalism, Nagao claims, has started to rot from within. The overemphasis on individualism, personal happiness, and social contracts has begun to destroy the final unit of social organization—the family—weakening the bonds of marriage and the bonds between parents and children. The traditional American enterprising spirit has been eroded by rampant consumer lust, as have patterns of saving and investment. "American-style management," he concludes, "continues to constantly alienate the work force and is thus doomed to fight a losing battle with Japanese corporations that enjoy the concentrated energies of their legions of employees."[22]

Shuji Umano: The America Basher

Nagao is a reasoned critic, but just as America has its Japan bashers, Japan also has a few real America bashers. Of them, Shuji Umano is definitely on the extreme fringe. A member of the prewar generation and a Shinto nationalist, he not only subscribes to the view that America's collapse is a historical necessity, but he believes that America is an intrinsically "evil" force in the world and that Japan and America are archenemies. He has written nearly twenty books with titles such as "The Decline of America," "The Final War Between Japan and America," and "Predicting U.S.-Japan Reversal: Revealing the Inevitability of History."

Umano is the sort of emotional writer, somewhere between lucid and lunatic, that one encounters fairly frequently in Japan in certain genres of popular literature. In his 1985 book *Gijutsu bunmei no hosoku* [Principles of a Technological Civilization], he argues that military rivalries are essentially obsolete, that technology is the true force shaping the world economy, and that the center of this force is Japan. The key to modern civilization, he says, is the ability to generate and collect information, and because Japanese society is homogeneous and has a uniform level of education and living patterns, it will best be able to take advantage of the post-industrial information age. American society is doomed because it is fundamentally anti-information, plagued with illiteracy and internal frictions so that information flows only from the top down and is distorted. America is also so militarized that a great deal of its information exists within a "black box," accessible only to specialists. American society is also decadent and arrogant, with citizens—descendants of Europe's lower classes—who still have a servile respect of Europe but a sense of racial superiority toward the Japanese and Russians.[23]

In 1992 Umano translated an unpublished report by the CIA titled *Japan 2000*—a leaked document nearly as paranoid and critical of Japan as Umano is of the United States. In the wide-ranging annotations and opinions he supplied, Umano noted (in addition to the fact that the American flag has the same number of stripes as the number of steps that General Tojo ascended to the gallows when the Americans hanged him after World War II) that the United States and the Soviet Union were like Siamese twins, and that if one dies, the other must, too. Like the former Soviet Union, the United States (controlled by Jewish Illuminati conspirators) is a monotheistic society, and this same monotheism has been behind almost all the evils in the world. A characteristic of societies believing in a single almighty god, he says, is a rigid social hierarchy whereby a few enormously wealthy families use their servant classes (dogs) to control the masses of people (sheep), who have no rights at all; the extreme form of this is slavery. Democracy, according to Umano, is only a mechanism to give the illusion of equality to the lower classes, who are given hardly anything, no matter how hard they work. As a result people shirk work and rarely assume responsibility for it. Since Japan is pantheistic, human-based, with no clear spiritual hierarchy, its people work hard because they know that by contributing to society they are contributing to themselves.[24]

As the English-language title of one of his other books, *Civilization Evolved from Japan*, suggests, Umano believes civilization first appeared in Japan and traveled West, to China, India, the Middle East, Europe, and the United States, and that as it has traveled it has become more impure and distorted (possessing more entropy), and more evil. Unlike Japan, which has been able to preserve the essence of an ancient culture and retain its genetic and spiritual purity, the United States is overrun with different races and cultures, which generate only more "entropy" and evil. America, Umano says, "is the graveyard of civilization."[25]

In Umano's belief system one can see traces of the prewar propaganda line that Japan is a unique, divinely destined nation with a racially and spiritually pure people, in contrast to America, which is a confused and decadent mongrel nation and therefore doomed. What makes Umano both interesting and disturbing is that he is no ordinary right-wing crackpot. He is a former MITI official who once lived in the United States and taught chemical engineering at the Polytechnic Institute of New York. By no means a household name in Japan, he would certainly be regarded with amused embarrassment by many. Nonetheless, his theories clearly resonate with many readers, for they continue to buy his books, almost all of which are issued by major publishers.

The Racial Mirror

Subcurrents of thought similar to Umano's are also found in writings that focus on supposed Jewish-American conspiracies to take over the world. Far-fetched as these theories are, however, some have far more complex roots than borrowed prewar Nazi ideology. There are almost no Jews in Japan, and despite having been allied with Germany in World War II, Japan has little history of anti-Semitism. During the war several Japanese government officials even helped save thousands of European Jews from the Nazi maw.

As noted earlier in this book, some of the Jewish conspiracy theories in Japan reflect admiration of, even a twisted identification with, Jewish people. This is true of some of the most rabidly anti-Jewish writers, such as Masami Uno, head of the "Liberty Information Institute" and a one-man industry with books like *Yudaya to tatakatte, sekai ga mieta* [In Fighting the Jews, the World Came into Focus]. In 1992 Uno authored *Kodai yudaya wa Nippon ni fuin sareta* [Ancient Jewry Is Sealed in Japan], which suggests that the ark of the covenant was brought to Japan, that the lost tribes of Israel mixed with ancient Japanese, and that many of today's Japanese—not the "white Jews"—are the true descendants of Abraham. The book went through eleven printings in six months.

Many of the most paranoid anti-Jewish themes do not originate in Japan but are imported from the United States. In the summer of 1993, ads for three anti-Jewish books appeared in Japan's most prestigious newspapers. The ads were attacked by representatives of the Simon Wiesenthal Center in Los Angeles and other rights groups. The controversy was widely reported in the U.S. media, but there was almost no mention of the American connection. Titled *Saigo no kyoteki Nihon wo ute: yudaya sekai shihai no puroguramu* [Strike The Last Real Enemy, Japan: The Jewish Program for World Domination], the books were emblazoned with subtitles proclaiming that Japan's Ministry of Finance and the Bank of Japan are already controlled by Jews and that nearly all of Japan's problems are the result of a global Jewish conspiracy. Although almost certainly written by a Japanese, they were purportedly "translations" of a work by an American named Jacob Morgan.[26]

Hideo Levy, an expatriate and the only American to ever win the prestigious Noma Prize for his literary writings in Japanese, commented on Japan's anti-Jewish phenomenon in a 1988 essay. Noting that one particularly anti-Jewish book had sold over a hundred thousand copies, he writes, "It seemed odd to me. There was absolutely no logical reason for discrimination against Jews—one of the traditional sicknesses of Western civilization—to manifest itself in Japan. When I checked into the matter, I discovered that the Japanese author was a member of a fundamentalist Christian sect centered in the American south. Indeed, it appeared that behind the anti-Jewish phenomenon in Japan was actually one of the more ridiculous examples of a Japanese person putting on Western airs, imitating the rural religion of America's least educated poor whites (the type found in abundance among supporters of the anti-Japanese congressman Richard Gephardt)."[27]

This same phenomenon—of American prejudices reflected in Japanese attitudes toward Americans—is not limited to anti-Jewish books. In the early 1990s, several famous Japanese cartoonists were accused of promoting images offensive to African-Americans; a letter-writing campaign by churches and schools in the United States, coordinated by a Japanese group, deluged Japanese publishers and the artists with demands for censorship of the comics. Some were withdrawn from the market, and others were published with disclaimers, but most of the Japanese artists were horrified and confused when they were accused of being racists. Like purveyors of black "winkie" and "sambo" dolls and other racially offensive items often found for sale in Japan, they had merely adopted most of the images years ago from the United States along with everything else.

To examine racial attitudes in Japan today is to enter a hall of mirrors. Japanese comics and animation artists have appropriated not only American racist imagery; in the postwar period, after the humiliating defeat of World War II and the resulting loss of national self-confidence, artists began drawing Japanese with an idealized but distinctly "Caucasian" look. Although this tendency is softening as Japanese regain their self-confidence, in girls' comics Japanese females are often still drawn on covers with "blond" hair and big "blue" eyes. When Chinese or other Asians are depicted in comics, however, they are often rendered with slanted eyes and buck teeth— the same sort of imagery white U.S. artists once used in less enlightened times to depict Japanese and Chinese people. As for black and white foreigners, in Japanese comics for women they are often depicted as fashion models. In comics for men they are often depicted as enormous, oversexed, and thick-lipped or hairy brutes.

Are Japanese people particularly racist? It is certainly understandable if many Americans think so, considering the racially insulting remarks some high Japanese officials have made in recent years and the negative press Japan has received as a result. Many Japanese do tend to view the world in racial terms, and when talking to foreigners they will usually stress that Japan is "racially homogeneous." This is the official line. But almost all Japanese today know they are really a mixture of several different ethnic groups. In a relaxed setting young people will often look at each other's faces and joke about appearing "Polynesian," "Southeast Asian," "Korean," or "from the continent" (meaning China). If someone is a little hirsute, they may even gingerly mention "Russians" or "Ainu" (Japan's indigenous, proto-Caucasoid race).

There is a real danger in applying simplistic U.S. notions of racism to a country like Japan, however. Japan has never codified racism or discrimination based on skin color into its legal system, as has the United States. And the most pernicious discrimination in Japan is actually not against other races, but against the *burakumin*, or Japan's former "untouchable" class, and against ethnic Korean residents, both of whom (despite what Japanese claim) are racially indistinguishable from the general population. The Japanese "anti-Jewish" phenomenon, for that matter, may actually be an indirect way of expressing resentment against foreigners in general. As if to support this theory, in the spring of 1993 when ultra-right-wing groups tacked up posters throughout Tokyo calling for expulsion of "illegal immigrants," the posters were emblazoned with Nazi swastikas.[28]

What seems to be racial discrimination in Japan often stems more from language and cultural problems than from race; it is often a type of "ethnicism." Even African-American John G. Russel, who in 1991 wrote a badly needed book for the Japanese market titled *Nihonjin no kokujinkan: mondai wa "Chibikuro Sambo" dake de wa nai* [Japanese Views of Blacks: The Problem Isn't Just "Little Black Sambo"], notes that for all the Caucasian prejudice against blacks and other people of color that Japan has absorbed, he does not feel comfortable calling it a "racist" society." After interviewing a variety of blacks living in Japan, he writes, "one comes to the conclusion that in Japan there is little of the hatred of blacks that one often encounters in the West; on the contrary, the most striking thing is ignorance and arrogance."[29]

Both African-Americans and Euro-Americans may encounter racial slights or discrimination in Japan, but it is usually the Caucasians who howl the loudest, probably because they are not used to it. Caucasians have historically been put on a pedestal in Japan, and fair-haired, fair-skinned models still grace magazine covers and star in TV commercials, but as with all foreigners it is not uncommon for them to be turned down when renting an apartment.

Ultimately, whether the discrimination in Japan comes from ignorance and from inexperience in dealing with outsiders, or whether it is home-grown or imported, to the people being discriminated against the result is the same. It should be condemned, and ideally by enlightened Japanese. By America's standards, however, the Japanese brand of racism or "ethnicism" is nothing if not original.

A time in Japan can make Americans of all hues rethink cherished notions about themselves. At the end of the nineteenth century, the American William E. Griffis, who was quite progressive for his class, wrote in *The Romance of Conquest* that "Nothing can restrain the pushing ardor of the Anglo-Saxon, who believes that God formed the earth to be inhabited."[30] But in *The Mikado's Empire*, which he wrote after a year's sojourn in Japan, he could also say that "My eyes have not altered their angle, yet I see as the Japanese see. The 'hairy' foreigners are ugly. . . . How ugly those blue eyes! How deathly pale many of them look! . . . The white people are as curious, as strange, as odd, as the Japanese people themselves."[31]

Japanese Admirers of America

Most Japanese people have a genuine affection for Americans and admire the things Americans like to be admired for—being open, friendly, generous, and straightforward. Beyond their generalizations about "friendly people" and their infatuation with blue jeans—what do they admire about the United States, the nation?

In 1992, after one of the regular downturns in U.S.-Japan relations, the *Asahi* newspaper ran an article on Japanese feelings toward America.

It described how many people were feeling increasingly exasperated by the growing tensions between the two nations, and it featured short interviews with representatives of three postwar generations, highlighting the differences in their opinions.

Nobuyuki Nakahara, a fifty-seven-year-old president of a major corporation, had been an exchange student in the United States at the end of the 1950s when America was still the undisputed economic, political, military, and scientific leader of the world. A member of the generation raised in poverty and fed a diet of U.S. movies that depicted America as a materialistic paradise, he remembered his sense of awe just at the sight of freeways. "In pursuing an ideal human society based on freedom, equality, and charity, and based on the principles of its constitution," he says, "America has opened its gates to immigrants." This, he goes on to note, has made it a difficult country to govern; whereas corporations could once hire just on the basis of ability, now they have to fulfill quotas for minorities. The pendulum has swung from freedom to equality, he says, and that has indirectly led to protectionism directed at Japan. Nonetheless, he concludes, Japan should respect a nation like the United States, which stresses free trade, because it is in Japan's long-term interest to do so.[32]

Yukio Hatoyama, a forty-five-year-old member of the then ruling Liberal Democratic Party, had been an exchange student at Stanford University during the turbulent early 1970s, and he recalled that American science and technology were preeminent back then, but Japanese consumer products and cars were already gaining fast. He decided to become a politician and work for his own nation because he was inspired by the American patriotism and idealism he saw during this period. "Because America is a racial melting pot," he writes, "it has fostered a level of humanitarianism unprecedented in history. Problems manifest themselves in ways such as America's difficulty in competing economically with Japan and the riots in Los Angeles, but the true strength of America is its pursuit of an ideal society."[33]

Keiko Koshino, a thirty-two-year-old employee of the Bank of Tokyo, had worked in New York during 1990. A member of the generation raised in American-style affluence and less likely to be impressed by American's standard of living or technology, she had a more jaundiced view of the United States. She commented on homeless people and poor service in stores and found little to respect materially. Ultimately, however, she said, "I still like America, though. I like the fact that it's a society that accepts differences and lets people speak their minds so clearly."[34]

Later in the same year the paper ran a separate series of similar interviews, titled "My America." Misuzu Tamaru, a popular forty-one-year-old television newscaster who spent several years as a child and as an adult student in the United States, expressed her admiration for the U.S. political system. Noting the political passivity that exists in Japan as a result of the legacy of feudalism, she said, Japanese people "have very little consciousness of the need to hold up the nation, to object to government, or to monitor it, whereas in the United States people believe that the government exists for the people, and that they can change their leaders whenever they want."[35]

John Lennon's widow, Yoko Ono, was also interviewed in the same series. Commenting that the United States is a nation of dramatic change, she said that "one of the strengths of the U.S. is that if people believe it is the logical and right thing to do, they will accept something new without hesitation. And the constitution has a firm base in people's consciousness and lives, so that whenever the constitution or individual rights are violated, people rise up on their own." Recalling that John Lennon's song "Imagine" envisioned a world where people of different races and religion could live together without discrimination, she says, "We confirmed the dream and the ideal in American society. America is a very complicated place, with many different races, but all things considered, I think it does quite well. Sometimes it makes a mistake, like Vietnam. But I think it is a society that tries to live faithful to its ideals."[36]

What comes across here, from both critics and admirers of America, is a sense of how radically "different" America still seems to them—not so much in a material or physical sense as in its ideals, openness, and diversity (especially racial diversity) and in the system that makes it all possible.

Civilization versus Culture

In the mid-1980s, Ryotaro Shiba, one of Japan's most popular and respected historical novelists, made a forty-day whirlwind tour of the United States. He had never visited it before, he says, because he had always felt Japan was already so Americanized and he had been exposed to so many American films and books that it wasn't necessary. His experiences and observations were serialized and later compiled into a now classic book titled *Amerika sobyo* [Sketches of America]. Writing a book about a foreign nation based on a forty-day tour seems rather irresponsible, but Shiba—a former officer in the old Imperial army and a specialist in Japanese and Asian history—brought a remarkably open mind to his subject.

In his travels, Shiba associated with a wide variety of Americans and made observations from his perspective as both a Japanese and a historian. People, he says, are social beings who naturally form groups, and these groups are supported by "civilization" and "culture." "Civilization" Shiba defines as something "universal, logical, and functional, that anyone can participate in." "Culture," on the other hand, is something illogical and nonuniversal that only applies within a specific group, such as a race or tribe, but gives people emotional solace and a sense of identity. "Civilization" is exemplified by, for example, a traffic light, which everyone all over the world knows how to use, whereas "culture" is represented by a Japanese woman in kimono who always opens a sliding paper door by kneeling on a tatami mat and carefully opening the door with both hands—even when it might be easier to open it standing up. The United States, Shiba says, is a "civilization." It is an artificial nation created by laws, as compared to Japan, Ireland, Korea, or even Spain and most of the nations of Europe, which are essentially "cultures." In fact, almost all people around the globe live oppressively immersed in what are basically "cultures." The discovery of the New World in the fifteenth century was like a breath of fresh air in the Old World, and with the creation of the United States, a space in the world was created where nearly everyone could participate regardless of "culture."[37]

Shiba does not claim that America is made up of people with no culture and no sophistication (no history!) and is therefore inferior to Japan and other monoracial societies. This has been the traditional fall-back argument of Japanese nationalists and racial supremacists. At the same time, Shiba realizes that the "culture" he talks about—the identification with a small group or race or common history and customs—is an important part of human existence and one that many Americans crave in their lives.

True "civilizations," according to Shiba, only occur rarely in history. And they usually occur in places that can attract, absorb, and support populations of people who interact with their different cultures and expertise, take the best from each other, and eventually create a universal culture in which anyone can participate. It happened before, he says, in the Chou and Yin dynasties of ancient China, but the United States has done in two hundred years what took China thousands of years, and it is perhaps the only true "civilization" of the twentieth century. America is by no means a perfect civilization, he notes, and it is plagued by a persistent bad habit of trying to get other nations, which possess none of the conditions it has, to "become like America." Nonetheless, America incorporates one of the greatest strengths of multiethnic civilizations: ideas which emerge from one ethnic group are filtered through the sensibilities of all, and what results—whether jazz or jeans—has a universality that enables it to spread throughout the rest of the world.[38]

The Analogy of the Computer

Using some of the same types of generalizations that Japanese often make, we can speculate on the advantages America has that it might exploit in its economic competition with Japan. One way we can do this is through the analogy of the computer—the mind amplifiers that are a hallmark of modern American "civilization" (as Shiba might call it). Computers are one of the most revolutionary technologies ever created. They were developed and popularized in the United States, and they are one of the main areas of technology where the U.S. still has a considerable lead over Japan. Technoliterate Americans today often use computer terminology to further a mechanistic view of humans, jokingly referring to their brains as "CPUs" or their memory as "volatile." Because of the complexity of computer systems, however, computers may be even more suited as a focal point for discussing human societies.

Open versus Closed Systems

When comparing their society with that of the United States, Japanese people often say, almost apologetically, that theirs is *heisateki*, or "closed," compared to America's, which is "open." This same comparison is drawn about people, because Japanese often see themselves as bound by protocol, hierarchy, and formality, and are amazed at how freely Americans can speak their minds (and even talk to total strangers).

Openness is a characteristic not only of American society, but of American computer systems. In the computer world, until recently most system designs were proprietary and "closed," which meant the hardware and software of one manufacturer would work only with other products of the same manufacturer. Today, and this is especially true of the personal computer world, the overwhelming trend is toward "open systems" based on widely accepted standards—toward systems that allow equipment made by a variety of manufacturers to be connected together and that are designed so that anyone can manufacture equipment or write software for them. The result has been a synergy and an explosion in computer use, as more and more software and hardware manufacturers use economies of scale to bring their costs down and make their products affordable to users.

During the 1980s, Japanese personal computer manufacturers seemed able to do no wrong, and for a time it appeared as though they might devour their American competitors. But at the beginning of the 1990s, the trend reversed, and American hardware and software companies finally started to make inroads into the Japanese market. One of the reasons for this (in addition to the fact that Americans finally realized there was a lot of money to be made in Japan and started writing programs with Japanese-language capability) was that most American firms had been steeled in the fire of open competition. The U.S. computer industry, both hardware and software, is one of America's most fierce and unregulated, and because it has grown up around an open-system standard—primarily the IBM standard—it has had to compete in a huge marketplace against Japanese, European, Taiwanese, Korean, and other American firms. As a result it has become extraordinarily competitive in quality and price.

In contrast, the Japanese personal computer industry has until recently been protected in its home market by a language barrier that helped keep out foreign software, by a relatively "closed" distribution system, and by the tendency of Japanese hardware manufacturers to cling to their own designs. The Japanese never adopted a single open standard (which meant that they and the software creators were never able to enjoy large economies of scale in the domestic market). The industry was, in short, operating in a sheltered environment. Prices were too high, and companies were uncompetitive internationally.

At the beginning of the 1990s the walls surrounding the Japanese personal computer world started to crumble. The catalyst was the computer-telecommunications revolution. Savvy Japanese, following instructions printed in popular computing magazines, began using facsimile machines and phones to buy software and even whole computers directly by mail order from the United States, thus bypassing the entire Japanese distribution system. American manufacturers, for their part, began discovering how to sell computers in Japan, and American programmers started to write software for the Japanese market. The result, around 1991, was the beginning of an American-instituted computer price war in Japan—a complete role reversal for Japanese and American industries. By mid-1993, one Japanese computer columnist even speculated that local software developers might be reduced to mere translation companies, forced to do nothing but rewrite American English-language products for the Japanese market.[39]

It is this openness of the American system that in the long run can be one of our greatest strengths. America has historically been a wide-open nation, not just in computers, but in trade, in communication, in business, immigration, and in thought. This makes America a sometimes chaotic, unsettling, exhausting, even frightening place in which to live, but it is also responsible for enormous synergies of energy and creativity. Rather than shut ourselves off from new ideas, or hide behind barriers, the computer analogy suggests we would do well to make ourselves more open and throw ourselves into the fire of competition.

Horizontal versus Vertical Integration

In 1967, sociologist Chie Nakane wrote a now-classic book titled *Tate-shakai no ningen kankei* [Personal Relationships in a Vertical Society], later published in English as *Japanese Society*. Nakane's central theme was that nearly all relationships in Japan are characterized by a strong vertical hierarchy—not that Japan is ridden with class conflicts, but that in contrast to the United States and other Western nations Japan has almost no horizontal or truly equal relationships.

In the computer world, until recently, systems with many users were also hierarchical and organized around a giant central computer called a "mainframe." At first each user had to physically come to the computer to use it. Then, later, multiple users were connected to the central computer so they could access it through terminals or screens from a remote location, the central computer doling out its favors to each user as required. Now the trend is for systems to be organized in a more horizontal structure. Instead of being connected to giant mainframes occupying entire rooms, multiple users now have their own powerful personal computers, each one with its own "intelligence" and processing power, and these are hooked together in elaborate networks. Each user can communicate with the others on an equal basis—like a group of people in a room having a discussion using a facilitator instead of a centralized leader.

This reflects a larger trend in advanced societies. For many years, society seemed to be moving toward greater centralization, partly as a result of technology. Individuals formed tribes, tribes formed city-states, city-states formed nation-states, and nation-states centralized power with armies, schools, and standard languages. Information became more and more centralized, too, collected in books, libraries, and schools. Large corporations were organized with power radiating from headquarters down to the man or woman in the field in a clear hierarchy. As culture became more and more homogeneous, as people in each nation started watching the same television shows, reading the same news, and driving the same car, even thoughts became "centralized."

Now the trend may be shifting in the other direction. Because of changes in communications and computer technology, we no longer all have to watch the same one or two television channels but can choose from among a hundred. With telephone lines and faxes and computers and modems, more and more people can leave the major cities and work at home or wherever they please. When energy becomes decentralized— as it surely will be in the very near future thanks to solar energy and other types of power—this trend will only accelerate. At the same time, knowledge and intelligence are becoming more diffuse. Digitalization of information increasingly means that text, pictures, and sound can be copied instantly and stored where anyone can access and manipulate it.

All this means that instead of having to conform, people will find it easier and easier to maintain their individuality of thought while remaining part of a larger community. People will have to learn to relate to each other "horizontally"—as different but equal—unlike in a vertical social organization that almost always demands conformity. In the twenty-first century, therefore, the most dynamic and strong societies may be those best able to respect individualism and diversity—to be decentralized, but with all the social connections intact.

If U.S. society can avoid disintegrating (or falling into what Shuji Umano might call a maximum state of entropy), it is ideally positioned to use technology to further horizontally integrate itself. Our telephone network gave us first voice and then fax communication; now, with personal computers attached to the network, horizontal communication is exploding across vast spaces. Observing the spontaneous communication that increasingly takes place on commercial and semipublic computer networks (such as the vast, amoebalike Internet)—where millions of ordinary people now furiously type messages back and forth to each other every day, completely oblivious to social hierarchy and to differences in race, sex, sexual orientation, or even physical handicaps—one cannot help thinking that this is an extraordinarily American sort of phenomenon and one that should be exploited to competitive advantage.

In this sense, the February 22, 1993 proposal made by President Clinton and Vice-President Gore for investment in a national "information superhighway"—a high-speed computer network that would allow ideas, data, and images to move around the country far faster and easier than they do now—is one of the most exciting ideas ever to emerge from our government. In the same tradition as the federal government's promotion of national communication through railway and highway systems, it is a relatively low-cost investment that holds out the promise of vastly improved communication and savings in energy as well as new synergies in human knowledge. And it will further strengthen one of America's greatest assets—the horizontal integration of our society.

The vertical orientation of Japan—its hierarchy and protocols—makes for a very tidy and gracious society, but it also imposes a tremendous burden. What kind of burden? A poster for employees in a train station gives an example. It used pictures to show how many degrees to bow to customers in six different situations:

1. The "Welcome" bow—30 degrees.
2. The "Yes" bow, when answering in response—15 degrees.
3. The "Please go ahead" bow—15 degrees.
4. The "Apology" bow—45 degrees, but 60 degrees for deep regret.
5. The "Sorry-to-keep-you-waiting" bow—30 degrees.
6. The plain "Thank you" bow—45 degrees.

The point here is not that Americans can gain advantage by being rude, but that in American business, in particular, the horizontal integration, the decentralization, and the lack of hierarchy allow for considerable flexibility. Employees can come together quickly to form temporary, informal associations and even "virtual corporations," where they interact with each other more or less as equals. In smaller firms, especially, flexibility allows employees to make decisions far faster than their Japanese counterparts, who must wade through a swamp of protocols and hierarchies and carefully establish a consensus before deciding to act.

"Software" versus "Hardware"

Japanese people often say that America is strong in "software" whereas Japan is strong in "hardware." In the strict sense, they mean that the United States is better at creating software programs for computers, but that Japan leads the United States in manufacturing the computer's mechanical components.

Like most generalizations, this one steamrolls over important exceptions. For example, Japan completely dominates the world today in the entertainment software American children love, and the U.S. firm Intel has a near monopoly in the manufacture of the microprocessors that are the brains of modern personal computers. Nonetheless, the generalization is true when it comes to business and scientific and engineering software. The larger size of the U.S. software industry, its greater experience, and its basis in the English language give American software developers a clear advantage.

Software is one industry where United States companies can exploit their advantage to great profit through exports to Japan. Much more aggressive targeting of the rapidly growing Japanese software market and more "localizing" of software—of tailoring it to Japanese tastes and business customs and language instead of assuming that everyone should do things the American way—is required. But software sales in Japan can help reduce the trade imbalance.

Software can also help improve the balance of trade by reducing our imports. It is not immediately obvious to most of us, but software, in conjunction with computer chips, is increasingly substituting for hardware—for the functions of complex mechanical mechanisms and physical switches. Wristwatches, which not too long ago contained scores of springs and gears, now often have no moving parts at all. Computers that once filled entire rooms can now fit in a person's hand and perform even more functions.

In earlier years, Japan—like most developing nations—practiced a deliberate form of import substitution to save scarce foreign exchange. Instead of importing goods, Japan developed industries that could supply the same products locally. Today the United States has a chance to reduce its imports from Japan by substituting software functions for imported hardware.

The facsimile machine is an example. The Japanese-made fax machines in nearly all American offices today contribute a sizable portion to our trade deficit. Yet almost the entire physical fax machine can be replaced today by a few computer chips (made by Rockwell and ATT, among others) and an American-made software package installed on an

American-made personal computer—which most offices already have. Every software fax system installed means one fewer physical device or machine likely to be imported from Japan.

The same software advantage can be utilized in the future in a variety of fields. As computers and telecommunications merge, VCRs will disappear, to be replaced by digital movies that run on "computers." Dials and switches on autos, stereos, or anything that currently uses a physical control panel will also probably disappear, to be replaced by virtual switches projected on programmable touch-screen displays. When television goes digital and is hooked up to communications networks, the computer will not only be a television but a two-way picture phone—which is why it is absolutely imperative that American industry become competitive in display devices. Eventually, because we won't have to travel so often to get information, and because we will be able to do much of our work from home, computers and software will be able to reduce the number of cars we need and even the amount of oil we have to import. The possibilities for American industry in the digital age—if it takes advantage of the U.S.'s strengths in software and the U.S.'s huge installed base of computers—are thrilling.

There is another, broader sense in which Japanese also say the United States is "strong in software." *Sofuto*, or "software," in Japanese today means not only computer programs but movies, books, and music—almost any nonphysical idea or intellectual property, as opposed to the physical devices used to store, access, or display it. Matsushita's purchase of MCA and Universal Studios, Sony's purchase of Columbia Pictures, and the heavy investment in U.S. research laboratories by Japanese companies are all attempts by Japanese hardware manufacturers to obtain the "software" they lack—the movies and music that play on their video machines, laser disk players, and Walkmans, as well as the ideas they need for their next generation of products.

This is not meant to imply that Japanese people are innately noncreative. Anyone who has read Japanese comics or watched Japanese movies knows better than that. But Japanese social structure—particularly corporate structure, with its emphasis on hierarchy, loyalty, and conformity—is not always conducive to the adoption of radically new ideas. As Ryotaro Shiba implied, because of Japan's relative homogeneity and island nature and the lack of different races intermingling with each other and filtering each other's ideas, it may be harder for Japanese people to come up with truly "universal" ideas.

The message here is that "soft" power may be more important than "hard" power. Ultimately America's greatest strength is its ideology—the belief, centered around the U.S. Constitution, in individual freedoms and human equality. Our syncretic and multicultural society, the synergies we obtain from it, and the visions and dreams that result from these synergies—which may lead us into the frontiers of outer space, data space, biotechnology, and the ocean depths—are a reason we are a world power, far above and beyond our military might or our physical wealth.

Systems Management

Systems are regularly interacting or interdependent people or things that are organized to form a unified whole and to work together. Systems management is what makes complex computer networks, telephone systems, or airline systems possible, and the difference between good and bad systems management is obvious to anyone who has ever tried to use a telephone or board an airplane in a large airport in a developing nation.

Systems management is another way of looking at what Ryotaro Shiba called America's "civilization." One of the things that distinguishes the United States from so many other nations and makes our society work well, in his view, is that it is an artificial creation supported almost entirely by laws. The laws in this case begin with the legal rights defined in the U.S. Constitution and percolate down through the legal system to the grassroots of our society. To Americans this may all seem second nature, but the American experiment is unique, and systems management is what gives it universal potential.

Japanese businessmen and engineers often refer to the United States as being a *keiyaku* (contract) or a *manyuaru* (manual) society. They frequently use these words in a pejorative sense, out of the frustration that occurs when they have to use American lawyers to negotiate agreements or work with American factory employees who insist on minor procedures in unwieldy manuals. In Japan many business agreements are still made orally, and businesses and manufacturers still rely heavily on personal knowledge and know-how, transmitted not by written manuals but orally from person to person and by learning on the job.

Americans are often plagued by the same frustrations. We have to deal with so many lawyers and so many people who insist on "going by the book" that sometimes it seems as if our entire society will grind to a halt. But laws and contracts and manuals are the glue of modern American society. They are not sufficient to organize a society, for they do not teach people how to behave or have a sense of responsibility—that is the job of culture and schools and families—but they are what enable our systems to work in a society where not every participant has been raised with the same assumptions or the same body of knowledge.

One can see this at work in corporations. American businesses have a very high rate of employee turnover compared with Japan, yet they can continue to function because their method of doing business has usually been documented and codified into some sort of manual, and contracts have been exchanged with employees that carefully define and delineate their rights and responsibilities. To exaggerate, if all the employees of an American corporation were suddenly fired, and a new group hired the next day, it would be far easier for the American firm to continue to do business than for a Japanese corporation in the same situation. In Japan, if all the original workers were suddenly removed from the corporation and replaced, the corporation would probably cease to function. No one would know what to do.

The same can be said of the nation. If the present population of the United States were poured out, and a new population consisting of different races and cultures were poured in, society might continue to function as long as the new members could communicate with each other and read the "rules" or understand the "laws." America, in other words, would still be America. But in a similar situation the Japan we know would cease to exist.

The United States' strengths in systems management are visible in the areas in which we have had some of our biggest successes—in managing the Apollo program to put a man on the moon, in developing and managing the world's largest telecommunications network, in developing and managing our airline industry and the exploding new field of computer networks, and in operating huge multinational corporations. As we enter a globalized world, where we are forced on a daily basis to interact and work with different languages, cultures, and systems, this strength will become increasingly important. Systems management, and the ability to make diverse elements work together systematically as a cohesive, complex whole, is a hallmark of modern American civilization. It comes from the knowledge and experience we have in working with diversity. The next step is for us to take full advantage of all the diversity our people possess.

Feedback

In a world of dramatic change, the most robust societies are those with the best feedback systems. Feedback is used by both automatic machines and animals. It involves scanning behavior for its result and then modifying that behavior based on its success or failure. It is a crucial part of nearly every self-correcting mechanical device we use in modern society—from thermostats to computer disk drives—and it also appears in human behavior. Whenever we pick up a glass of water to drink, we rely on a steady feedback of visual and tactile information to make sure the water goes down our throats instead of being spilled on the floor. Feedback allows us to take actions, to see whether the results are successful, and to modify our behavior as needed.

Economies depend heavily on feedback. If the capitalist, free-market forms of government prevailed over communist command economies in the late twentieth century, it was not because they were morally superior but because they had better feedback systems. Businessmen in capitalist, free-market societies depend on feedback from the marketplace, usually in the form of sales receipts, to adjust prices, inventory, and designs to prevailing demand. In centralized, command economies like the former Soviet Union, one of the greatest problems is that the feedback system does not work properly, which creates imbalances in supply and demand. Factories produce unwanted goods, prices are unrelated to true costs, and there is little pressure for quality control. Productivity gains in the United States in the early 1990s are at least partly explained by improvements in feedback brought about by computer technology, by the use of bar code scanners, point-of-sale systems, and other means of transmitting sales information back to warehouses, factories, and headquarters.

Political systems also rely on feedback. History is replete with examples of societies where rulers became so divorced from the wishes of their subjects that they were violently overthrown. Particularly in large, complex societies, both the news media and free elections (and even demonstrations) play a critical role. They provide rulers with feedback on how policies are working and what people want, so they can respond and make corrections.

The economic and political systems of both Japan and the United States are superficially similar, but one of the great strengths of the United States is the superior feedback it enjoys. Japan may have one of the world's most smoothly functioning economies. Yet the problems Japan has with nearly all its trading partners are not just the result of its superior competitiveness. They are also the result of a malfunctioning feedback system in the domestic market—caused by consumers who lack power (or fail to exercise power) and inefficient distribution systems and cartels that hold up domestic prices and inhibit imports. These distortions are magnified by even worse problems in the political feedback system—by high-level officials involved in a never-ending series of scandals, ineffective opposition parties, an entrenched bureaucracy, and shadowy political dealmakers who seem to operate almost independent of the electorate. Japan is a dynamic and flexible society, but most of the changes it has experienced in recent history are still the result of external, not internal, pressure.

When Japanese people say they admire the U.S. political system, one of the things they are really referrring to is our unsurpassed feedback system and its ability for self-correction. There are distortions and imperfections in both the U.S. economic and political systems. For years, a large militarized part of our economy existed outside the normal feedback system. Persistent discrimination has until recently kept minorities out of the political system. And many people are so apathetic and disillusioned they do not even bother to vote. But as in our elections, which are an institutionalized alternative to violent revolution, when the U.S. system does work properly it permits a breathtaking degree of change.

Even Shuji Umano, who believes the United States to be the source of most of the evil in the world today, acknowledges this in a backhanded way. In his book *Civilization Evolved from Japan*, he declares that "Japanese society sometimes seems to change even faster than America, but the change takes a different form. Japan has roots that are unmovable, and what changes is only the branches and leaves above ground. American society in fact has no roots, and like the floating islands of Lake Titicaca in South America—which at first glance appear as though they could never budge—is moving in its entirety."[40]

Were Thomas Jefferson and other founders of the United States to observe our society today, they would probably faint at many of the changes we have wrought, but they would surely remain impressed with the way we have preserved their original revolutionary spirit. The United States is a fundamentally revolutionary society, and to survive it must remain so.

* * * * *

For Americans, Japan can be like a room of fun-house mirrors, where people enter, delight in the odd, distorted images they encounter, and then in the reflections see themselves.

The United States is not a fundamentally superior nation. Both Japan and America have their strengths and weaknesses, and they are uncannily similar in more ways than not. But by recognizing and reflecting on the differences in both societies we can establish a new frame of reference and a new perspective on our own reality, and improve ourselves as a result.

"[The Japanese] mind-photograph of the world," wrote Percival Lowell in 1888, "can be placed side by side with ours, and the two pictures combined will result beyond what either alone could possibly have afforded. Thus harmonized, they will help us to realize humanity."[41]

SUMMING UP

Several years ago I accompanied a Japanese software expert on a visit to some high-tech American firms in Silicon Valley. After the visit was over, he turned to me and smiled.

"You know what?" he said. "I finally understand why we Japanese could never have developed the computer. It has to do with religion."

"Oh, really?" I responded, bracing for a round of cultural generalizations.

"It's true," he continued. "Most computers use binary logic, and they calculate everything thing based on offs and ons, or zeroes and ones. It's exactly the sort of thinking one would expect to come from a Judeo-Christian culture. Judeo-Christian religions came out of the harsh desert environment of the Middle East, where it's easy to perceive reality in terms of a duality, of black and white, or good and evil. But in the lush islands of Japan, we don't think in dualities. We're a pantheistic society, and instead of black and white we see everything in shades of gray. But this is also one of our great strengths, because it's what gives us our enormous flexibility. And it explains why we Japanese are so enthusiastic about the new fuzzy logic system of mathematics. Just wait and see what we do with that!"

This man's observation was a strained, after-the-fact attempt to explain something very complex with a cultural generalization. But he had a point that relates, not to computers, but to this book.

As Americans, it is true that we tend to view the world in a dualistic way. Whether from the Judeo-Christian influence or not, we like to reduce things to an either-or, good-bad, yes-no, black-white, straight-gay, Republican-Democrat reality. But in dealing with Japan this type of thinking may not work well. Japan is a ferocious economic competitor, but it is not a military competitor (unless we want it to be). Japan may not always be a "friend," but that does not mean it is an "enemy." Japan's domestic market may not be completely "open," but that does not mean that it is completely "closed," either.

One could continue on and on along this line of argument, but the idea here is that Japan *is* a gray area in the American experience, and that it is this "grayness" itself that is a source of great frustration to many people. Without subscribing to the Japanese dogma of uniqueness, Japan *is* different from most other cultures Americans have dealt with until recently. It is one of the world's most economically and technologically powerful nations, superficially very similar to the United States and other industrialized nations, but not part of the European, Judeo-Christian tradition. It has been, and it is, a friend, a foe, a model, and a mirror—at different times and all at once. And this leads to some of the more important points I think we Americans would do well to remember in our dealings with Japan.

- Japan is merely a metaphor for the many other "different" cultures with which we will have to learn to live as equals. Japan was the first nation outside the Judeo-Christian, European tradition to fully industrialize, but today it is only one among many—having been joined by Singapore, Korea, Taiwan, and others. And Japan will soon be joined by China, and eventually India, and nations in Africa and Latin America, all of which will probably have adopted capitalist structures and modern technology, but tailored them to their own cultures and systems. The successes and the problems America has had in relating to Japan in trade and other areas are training for the future.

- As America and Japan grow closer and closer economically and culturally, the frequency of our arguments is likely to increase. This may not be a bad thing. A certain level of ideological competition is probably healthy, just as economic and technological competition is healthy. And in both America and Japan we may need opposing forces to define ourselves, motivate our citizens, and change our societies. But because in very recent history we were foes—mortal enemies—we need to be careful that the level of rhetoric used does not escalate beyond control. Having once shed blood, the patterns of conflict remain in our mutual memories and are all too easy to reactivate.

- America and Japan are both dynamic, rapidly changing societies; in our own ways, we are both "internationalizing." Many of the trade problems we face today are really the problems of a shrinking world. Just as Japan is being forced to adjust many aspects of its domestic economy to integrate it into the global economy, so, too, is America. We are learning how to export and compete better on the world market, and we are gradually changing our patent laws to conform to those of Japan and the rest of the world; eventually we will have to adopt the metric system, too. Both Japan and America are not monolithic entities, but aggregates of individuals, and many of the social problems that our peoples confront—the increase in social alienation, confusion, and even disintegration—are also the problems of a shrinking world and rapid changes in technology.

- America and Japan are wonderfully complementary cultures, capable of great synergies. Primarily because of computers, in biotechnology, energy, manufacturing, and information management, the world is entering a phase that will rival or even surpass the industrial revolution in its potential for good and its potential for social disruption. Both the United States and Japan are in the lead of this new revolution, and we would do well to further increase our level of cooperation, for at this point the problems created by technology—such as pollution—are only going to be solved by technology.

• Both Japanese and American societies are a fusion of old and new. Just as Japan has had to move culturally further and further from its Asian roots, so, too, is much of American culture starting to diversify beyond its European, Judeo-Christian roots and to incorporate more indigenous, African, Asian, and even more "Japanese" styles of thinking. Whether it is America teaching Japan about democracy and diversity, or Japan teaching America about competitiveness and cooperation, we almost seem to have been invented for each other.

NOTES

Introduction

1. Elizabeth Bisland, ed., *The Japanese Letters of Lafcadio Hearn* (Boston: Houghton Mifflin, 1910), p. 82.

One: Friend

Epigraph from Jack Kerouac, *The Dharma Bums* (New York: Viking Press, 1958), p. 203.

1. Van C. Gessel, "Postscript: Fact and Truth in The Samurai." In Shusaku Endo, *The Samurai* (New York: Harper and Row, 1982), p. 268.

2. Peter Booth Wiley (with Korogi Ichiro), *Yankees in the Land of the Gods: Perry and the Opening of Japan* (New York: Viking, 1990), p. 231.

3. Marco Polo, *The Book of Marco Polo* (copy with annotations by Christopher Columbus . . .), trans. Juan Gil (Madrid: Testimonio, 1986), pp. 84–86.

4. Filipe Fernandez-Armesto, *Columbus* (Oxford: Oxford University Press, 1991), p. 85.

5. Sanehide Kodama, *American Poetry and Japanese Culture* (Hamden, Connecticut: Archon Books, 1984), p. 8.

6. Foster Rhea Dulles, *Yankees and Samurai: America's Role in the Emergence of Modern Japan, 1791–1900* (New York: Harper and Row, 1965), pp. 1, 3–7.

7. Derek Massarella, *A World Elsewhere: Europe's Encounter with Japan in the Sixteenth and Seventeenth Centuries* (New Haven: Yale University Press, 1990), p. 349.

8. Hisakazu Kaneko, *Manjiro: The Man Who Discovered America* (Boston: Houghton Mifflin, 1956), pp. 95–97; and Dulles, *Yankees and Samurai*, p. 49.

9. Katherine Plummer, *The Shogun's Reluctant Ambassadors: Japanese Sea Drifters in the North Pacific* (Portland: Oregon Historical Society, 1991), pp. 77, 102–12.

10. William S. Lewis and Naojiro Murakami, eds., *Ranald MacDonald: The Narrative of His Early Life . . .* (Spokane: Eastern Washington State Historical Society, 1923), p. 120.

11. Ibid., pp. 264–65.

12. Townsend Harris, *The Complete Journal of Townsend Harris: First American*

Consul General and Minister to Japan (Garden City, New York: Doubleday, Dorand, 1930), p. 579.

13. Federal Communications Commission, Common Carrier Bureau, "Common Carrier Bureau—Statistics of Communications Carriers." (Does not include Mexico and Canada.)

14. Junko Takahashi, "Faasuto fuudo no owarinaki tatakai" [The Endless Fast Food Battle], *Asahi Shinbun Weekly Aera,* 24 September 1991, p. 72.

15. "Chrysler to Sell Mitsubishi Stake," *San Francisco Chronicle,* 3 July 1993, p. B2.

16. *Nikkei Kaisha Joho 93–II* [Nikkei Company Information 93-II] (Tokyo: Nihon Keizai Shinbun, Spring 1993), pp. 645–68.

17. Peter Hadfield, *Sixty Seconds That Will Change the World: The Coming Tokyo Earthquake* (Boston: Charles E. Tuttle, 1992).

18. Keizai Koho Center, *Japan 1993: An International Comparison* (Tokyo: Keizai Koho Center, 1993), p. 92.

19. Letter to author by Major N. J. LaLuntas, USMC, Deputy Director of Public Affairs, Headquarters, United States Forces, Japan, 11 August 1993; also, conversations with U.S. Army and Navy archivists, August 1993.

20. *World Almanac and Book of Facts, 1992,* p. 77.

21. Orna Feldman, "Amerikajin mo odoroku Amerika ganbo" [Even Americans Are Surprised by How Much People Want to Live in America], *Aera,* 18 February 1992, pp. 13–15; and Yukiko Ogura, "Green Card Lottery Offers Shot at American Dream," *Shukan ST,* 30 April 1993, p. 6.

22. Elfrieda Berthianme Shukart and Barbara Smith Scibetta, *War Brides of World War II* (Novato, California: Presidio Press, 1988), p. 217; and *Kodansha Encyclopedia of Japan* (Tokyo: Kodansha, 1983), Vol. 4, p. 271.

23. Masao Miyoshi, *As We Saw Them: The First Japanese Embassy to the United States (1860)* (Berkeley: University of Califonia Press, 1979), p. 172.

24. Yoshinori Shimizu, "Jobun" [Introduction]. In *Soba to kishimen* (Tokyo: Kodansha Bunko, 1989), pp. 79–105.

25. Deborah Boehm, "The Garbled Phrase as Frozen Music," *Spectator,* 4 January 1992, pp. 16–18.

26. Sanki Ichikawa, "Foreign Influences in the Japanese Language." In Inazo Nitobe et al., *Western Influences in Modern Japan: A Series of Papers on Cultural Relations* (Chicago: University of Chicago Press, 1931), pp. 141–80.

27. "Topics in the News," *City Limosine Bus,* Spring 1991, p. 33.

28. Kodama, *American Poetry and Japanese Culture,* p. 208.

29. Ibid., p. 13.

30. Earl Miner, *The Japanese Tradition in British and American Literature* (Princeton: Princeton University Press), p. 106.

31. Sanehide Kodama, ed., *Ezra Pound and Japan* (Redding Ridge, Connecticut: Black Swan Books, 1988), p. 249.

32. Interview with Daigaku at Hosshinji temple, Japan, 9 June 1992.

33. *Japanese Book News*, No. 2 (Spring, 1993), p. 1.

34. Peter Sanderson, "The Ronin Forum," *Amazing Heroes*, 15 June 1983, p. 44.

35. "Discussion Panel: 'Bande Dessinee,'" *Comics Journal*, March 1992, p. 80.

36. "American Culture Told in Numbers," *San Francisco Chronicle*, 2 November 1992, p. A6.

37. Kodama, *Ezra Pound and Japan*, p. 104.

38. "Tomaranai (?) Beikoku hihan: 'yunyu mokuhyochi' meguri tsugitsugi to" [Endless? Criticism of U.S.: Again and Again on Import Targets . . .], *Asahi Shinbun*, 1 June 1993, p. 7.

39. Joseph C. Grew, *Ten Years in Japan: A Contemporary Record Drawn from the Diaries and Private and Official Papers of Joseph C. Grew, United States Ambassador to Japan, 1932–1942* (New York: Simon and Schuster, 1944), p. 515.

40. John K. Emmerson, *A View From Yenan* (Washington, D.C.: Institute for the Study of Diplomacy, 1979), pp. 4, 40.

41. Zbigniew Brzezinski, "Europe and Amerippon: Pillars of the Next World Order," *New Perspective Quarterly*, Vol. 7, No. 2 (Spring 1990), p. 18.

Two: Foe

Epigraph from George Friedman and Meredith Lebard, *The Coming War With Japan* (New York: St. Martin's Press, 1991), p. 403.

1. William Elliot Griffis, *The Mikado's Empire* (New York: Harper and Brothers Franklin Square, 1895), pp. 367, 373.

2. Ibid., p. 350.

3. Raymond A. Esthus, *Theodore Roosevelt and Japan* (Seattle: University of Washington Press, 1966), pp. 37, 54.

4. Ibid., pp. 132–33.

5. Ibid., pp. 187–88.

6. Naoki Inose, "Nihonjin wa ima koso jibun no ronri wo kochiku suru toki da" [Now Is the Time for Japanese People to Form Their Own System of Logic], *Sapio*, 28 May 1992, pp. 18–20.

7. Inazo Nitobe, *The Works of Inazo Nitobe*, Vol. 4 (Tokyo: University of Tokyo Press, 1972), pp. 235, 265.

8. Dulles, *Yankees and Samurai*, p. 206.

9. Grew, *Ten Years in Japan*, p. 324.

10. John W. Dower, *War Without Mercy: Race and Power in the Pacific War* (New York: Pantheon Books, 1986), pp. 48–52, 60–71 .

11. Keizai Koho Center, *Japan 1993: An International Comparison*, pp. 6, 11, 65.

12. "Koreika no sokudo: Nippon ga sekai ichi" [Aging Population: Japan Is World's Fastest], *Asahi Shinbun*, 19 February 1993, p. 1.

13. Michael Abramowitz, "Japanese on Losing End of U.S. Real Estate Deals," *Washington Post*, 21 March 1992, p. 1.

14. Paul Krugman, *The Age of Diminishing Expectations: U.S. Economic Policy in the 1990s* (Cambridge: MIT Press, 1990), pp. 39–40.

15. Milton Friedman, "A Deficit That's Good for Us," *Washington Post*, 8 August 1993, p. C7.

16. Marc Levinson, "America's Edge," *Newsweek*, 8 June 1992, pp. 36–37.

17. "Nihon mo boeki fukosei shiteki" [Japan, Too, Can Point to Unfairness in Trade], *Asahi Shinbun*, 9 June 1992, p. 1.

18. "Invest in Japan, Trade Will Follow," *Business Week*, 14 June 1993, p. 130.

19. Shintaro Ishihara, *The Japan That Can Say No*, trans. Frank Baldwin (New York: Simon and Schuster, 1989), p. 21.

20. James Fallows, Chalmers Johnson, Clyde Prestowitz, and Karel van Wolferen, "Beyond Japan-bashing: The 'Gang of Four' Defends the Revisionist Line," *U.S. News and World Report*, 7 May 1990, p. 54.

21. "Miyazawa Says He Welcomes Pressure from Clinton on Trade," *San Francisco Chronicle*, 13 April 1993, p. 8.

22. Laurie M. Grossman and Michael J. McCarthy, "Hollings Invokes Hiroshima as Reply to Japanese Critic of U.S. Workers," *Wall Street Journal*, 4 March 1992, p. A2.

23. Friedman and Lebard, *The Coming War With Japan*, p. 403.

24. Sonni Efron, "A Cultural Trade Imbalance," *Los Angeles Times*, 21 May 1992, p. 1.

25. Hiroshi Hasegawa, "Nichibei kaisen hanseiki, genron hikaku: Doko ka nite imasenka?" [Comparing Views Half a Century after the Start of the U.S.-Japan War: Doesn't Something Seem Familiar Here?], *Aera*, 4 June 1991, pp. 32–35.

26. "Bei Keizai saisei no michi wa: Beinichi shikisha ni kiku" [Asking the Experts about the Road to a Revival in America], *Asahi Shinbun*, 1 March

1993, p. 7; and Akio Morita, "Shin-jiyu keizai e no teigen" [Proposal for a New Liberal Economy], *Bungei Shunju*, February 1992, pp. 94–109.

27. *Kodansha Encyclopedia of Japan*, Vol. 8, pp. 166–67.

28. "Pentagon Faults Japan over Defense Effort," *San Francisco Chronicle*, 6 October, 1992, p. A8.

29. "Japan and the United States: Teamwork Today and Tomorrow," (Japan: Ministry of Foreign Affairs, February 1993), p. 4; and "Asia's Arms Race: Gearing Up," *Economist*, 20 February 1993, pp. 19–20.

30. Kiyoaki Murata, ed., *Wa-Ei honyaku handobukku* [Japanese-English Translation Handbook] (Tokyo: Japan Times, 1971), p. 111.

31. David Lazarus, "Base Price: U.S. Bases in Japan Face an Uncertain Future," *PHP Intersect*, October 1992, p. 34.

32. Fred Hiatt, "Marine General: U.S. Troops Must Stay in Japan," *Washington Post*, 27 March 1990, p. A14.

33. Stan Kesser, "A Nation of Contradictions," *New Yorker*, 13 January 1992, p. 37.

34. Grew, *Ten Years in Japan*, p. 368.

35. "Tenno ochuji 'Okotoba' no kiiwaado wa" [Keywords in the Emperor's "Language" during Visit to China], *Asahi Shinbun*, 13 October 1992, p. 4.

36. Murata, *Wa-Ei honyaku handobukku*, p. 109.

37. Inose Naoki, *Mikado no Shozo* [A Portrait of the Mikado], Vol. 1 (Tokyo: Shinchosha, 1986), p. 19.

38. Takashi Ota, "Nihonsha dezain shinjidai: tomaranai 'shiro' ninki" [New Age of Japanese Car Designs: Relentless Popularity of "White"] *Nihon Keizai Shinbun*, 26 June 1986, p. 17.

39. Saburo Ienaga, *The Pacific War, 1931–1945* . . . (New York: Pantheon Books, 1978), p. 14.

40. Kyoko Isa, "Sosenkyo kekka: Jiminto no kakutoku giseki osugi, fuman" [Results of General Election: Dissatisfaction over LDP Gaining Too Many Seats], *Aera*, 3 August 1993, p. 18.

41. Hiroki Fukuda, "Jiminto sosaisen to uyoku to boryokudan: Takeshitaha no mazushiku sokoshirenu anbu" [LDP Leader Election, the Right Wing, and the Gangs: Takeshita's Pathetic, Endless Worries], *Aera*, 17 November 1992, p. 13.

42. David, E. Sanger, "A Japanese Major Suggests A Cure for Political Scandals," *New York Times*, 16 October 1992, p. A8; and "Rikujisansa wo chokai menshoku" [SDF Major Cashiered as Warning], *Asahi Shinbun*, 13 November 1992, p. 1.

43. "Books That Bash Are Latest Best Sellers," *Wall Street Journal*, 2 January 1991, p. B1.

Three: Model

Epigraph from Edmund G. Brown, Jr., "Why Can't America Be More Like Japan?," *California Magazine*, April 1985, p. 76.

1. Miner, *The Japanese Tradition in British and American Literature*, pp. 269–70.
2. Dulles, *Yankees and Samurai*, p. 222.
3. Bisland, *The Japanese Letters of Lafcadio Hearn*, p.254.
4. Griffis, *The Mikado's Empire*, p. 568.
5. Ibid., p. 570.
6. Dulles, *Yankees and Samurai*, p. 206.
7. Jay Mathews with Peter Katel, "The Cost of Quality: Faced with Hard Times, Business Tours on 'Total Quality Management," *Newsweek*, 7 September 1992, p. 49.
8. Interview with James N. Aliferis, San Francisco, 20 January 1993.
9. Stratford P. Sherman, "Japan's Influence on American Life," *Fortune*, 17 June 1991, p. 115.
10. L. Craig Parker, *The Japanese Police System Today: An American Perspective* (Tokyo: Kodansha International, 1984), p. 204.
11. Lafcadio Hearn, *Japan: An Attempt at Interpretation* (New York: MacMillan, 1904), p. 501.
12. Yoshio Yamanouchi, "Yakuza wo nakushite wa ikenai wake" [Why the Yakuza Must Not Be Eliminated], *Takarajima 30*, June 1993, pp. 130–38.
13. David E. Kaplan and Alex Dubro, *Yakuza: The Explosive Account of Japan's Criminal Underworld* (New York: MacMillan, 1986), p. 6.
14. Lance Morrow, "Japan in the Mind of America," *Time*, 10 February 1992, p. 19.
15. T. R. Reid, "Tokyo: U.S. Workers Outproduce Japanese," *Washington Post*, 7 February 1992, p. C1.
16. Interview with Satoshi Kamata, Tokyo, 19 June 1992.
17. Yumiko Ono and Jacob M. Schlesinger, "Land of Rising Fun: With Careful Planning, Japan Sets Out to Be a 'Life Style Superpower,'" *Wall Street Journal*, 2 October 1992, p. 1.
18. Atsushi Yamada, "'Hitsujigata soshiki' no byori: karoshi maneku yuto-seishudan no boso" [The Pathology of Sheep-style Organizations: Model Pupils Gone Berserk Invite Death from Overwork], *Aera*, 3 March 1992, p. 14.

19. Interview with Naoyuki Kameyama of the National Institute of Employment and Vocational Research, Tokyo, 31 March 1986.

20. Frederik L. Schodt, *Inside the Robot Kingdom: Japan, Mechatronics, and the Coming Robotopia* (Tokyo: Kodansha International, 1988), p. 160.

21. John Holusha, "Improving Quality, The Japanese Way," *New York Times*, 20 July 1988, p. D7.

22. Interview with Daigaku, 9 June 1992.

23. Schodt, *Inside the Robot Kingdom*, p. 66.

24. "Emperor's Letter from War End Disclosed," *Japan Times*, 16 April 1986, p. 1.

25. Stuart Auerbach, "The Ironies That Built Japan, Inc.: America's Cold War Leaders Helped Tokyo Curb Imports, Find Markets, Export Aggressively," *Washington Post*, 18 June 1993, p. 41.

26. Japan External Trade Organization, *The U.S. and Japan in Figures* (Tokyo: Jetro, 1991), p. 69.

27. Daniel I. Okimoto, *Between MITI and the Market: Japanese Industrial Policy for High Technology* (Stanford: Stanford University Press, 1989), p. 231.

28. David W. Schodt, "Internationally Traded Commodities as Dense Facts (Or Unpeeling the Banana)," paper presented before the Association for Integrative Studies, St. Paul, MN, 24–27 October 1991.

29. F. Schodt, *Inside the Robot Kingdom*, pp. 15, 130.

30. "Data Download," *ISRA News* (Newsletter of the International Service Robot Association), Spring 1993, p. 2.

31. Sam Jameson, "Market Scene: Japan's Companies Keep Factories—and Jobs—at Home," *Yomiuri Daily News*, 6 June 1992, p. 9A (L.A. Times World Report).

32. Ezra Vogel, *Japan as Number One: Lessons for America* (New York: Harper and Row, 1979), p. 117.

33. Akio Morita, "Shin-jiyukeizai e no teigen," [Proposal for a New Liberal Economy], *Bungei Shunju*, February 1993, p. 98.

34. "Computer Makers Win Ruling in Battle Over Screen Tariffs," *San Francisco Chronicle*, 31 December 1992, p. B4.

35. "Akaji de tsuppashiru ekisho senso" [Charging Ahead with Red Ink—The LCD Wars], *Aera*, 11 February 1992, p. 31.

36. Harold W. Stevenson and James W. Stigler, *The Learning Gap: Why Our Schools Are Failing and What We Can Learn from Japanese and Chinese Education* (New York: Summit Books, 1992), p. 223.

37. Vogel, *Japan as Number One*, p. 120.

38. Herbert Inhaber and Sidney Carrol, *How Rich Is Too Rich? Income and Wealth in America* (New York: Praeger, 1992), pp. 223–24.

39. Merril Goozner, "American Colleges Hit Hard by Charges of Fraud, Bankruptcy," *San Francisco Examiner*, 26 April 1992, p. B9.

40. Richard J. Samuels, "Facing Japan as a Technological Superpower," *MIT Japan Science and Technology Newsletter*, January 1993, p. 2.

41. T. R. Reid, "Japan Opens a New Chapter on Exports," *International Herald Tribune*, 29–30 August 1992; and Richard J. Samuels, "Facing Japan as a Technological Superpower," *MIT Japan Science and Technology Newsletter*, January 1993, p. 2.

42. "NASA Foreign Acquisitions Workshops, September 23–24, 1992," *Japanese Technical Literature Bulletin*, No. 16, September, 1992, p. 15.

43. "The Japanese Economy: From Miracle to Mid-life Crisis," *Economist*, SURVEY, 6 March 1993, p. 4.

44. Lester Thurow, *Head to Head: The Coming Economic Battle Among Japan, Europe, and America* (New York: William Morrow, 1992), pp. 289–90.

45. Postal Savings Bureau, Ministry of Posts and Telecommunications, *Mini Guide to Postal Service*, 1984, p. 6; and Ichiro Saito, "Kanemaru Noboru no guriin kaado tsubushi" [Noboru Kanemaru's Green Card Destruction], *Aera*, 23 March 1993, p. 10.

46. Clay Chandler, "Japan Official Stirs Up Debate on Postal Bank," *Wall Street Journal*, 16 December 1992, p. A10.

Four: Mirror

Epigraph from Bisland, *The Japanese Letters of Lafcadio Hearn,* p. 97.

1. Hearn, *An Attempt at Interpretation*, p. 10.

2. Percival Lowell, *The Soul of the Far East* (Boston: Houghton, Mifflin, 1888), p. 1.

3. Otis Port, "W. Edwards Deming and J. M. Juran: Dueling Pioneers," *Business Week* ("Quality"), 1991, p. 17.

4. Glenn A. Graham, *Automation Encyclopedia: A to Z in Advanced Manufacturing* (Dearborn, Michigan: Society of Manufacturing Engineers, 1988), p. 330.

5. Masaaki Imai, *Kaizen (Ky'zen), the Key to Japan's Competitive Success* (New York: McGraw Hill, 1986), p. 112.

6. Keisuke Tanaka and Toshiyuki Matsumoto, "Okyakusama daiichi wa mukashi kara dakedo, 'CS' da to nazeka moriagaru" ["Customer First" Has Been Around for Ages, But for Some Reason "CS" Is Taking Off], *Aera*, 2 July 1992, p. 74.

7. Jeffrey D. Shepard, "Japanese Leaders in Fuzzy Logic," *Byte*, April 1993, p. 116.

8. Andrew J. Pollack, "Cold Fusion, Derided in U.S., Is Hot in Japan," *New York Times*, 17 November 1992, p. C1.

9. Theodore Cohen, *Remaking Japan: The American Occupation as New Deal*, ed. Herbert Passin (New York: Free Press, 1987), pp. 11–12.

10. Kazuo Kawai, *Japan's American Interlude* (Chicago: University of Chicago Press, 1960), p. 30.

11. *Wa-Ei honyaku handobukku*, pp. 106–39.

12. Kawai, *American Interlude*, pp. 175, 177.

13. Paul R. Krugman, "Like It or Not, the Income Gap Yawns," *Wall Street Journal*, 21 May 1992, p. A13.

14. Interview, Joseph Engelberger, 30 January 1986.

15. Kizoshi Ogura, "Orenjizoku ni tsuite kataru ogura kizoshi: karera mo jukyo no kachikan hitei sezu" [Kizoshi Ogura on the 'Orange Tribe': They Do Not Reject Confucian Values], *Aera*, 26 January 1993, p. 9.

16. "Mayaku osen chiho toshi e" [Drug Contamination Reaches Regional Cities], *Asahi Shinbun*, 6 February, 1993, p. 30.

17. Usukura Kosuke, "Tai/Samuito—Hojin ryokoshara genkaku kinoko de sei-shinsakuran" [Japanese Travelers Develop Psychological Problems with Psychedelic Mushrooms in Thailand/Samui Island], *Aera*, 18 August 1992, p. 64; and Koichi Morizumi, "Media no fuunji Kadokawa Haruki no tenraku" [The Fall of Haruki Kadokawa, the Media's Lucky Gambler], *Aera*, 7 September 1993, p. 13.

18. Frederik L. Schodt, "Manga: Reflecting the Light and Dark Sides of Society," *Mainichi Daily News*, 21 November 1992, p. B9.

19. Naoyuki Agawa, *Amerika ga kirai desuka* [Do You Dislike America?] (Tokyo: Kodansha, 1993), p. 302.

20. Ruiko Yoshida, *Ruiko Yoshida no Amerika* [Ruiko Yoshida's America] (Tokyo: Kodansha Bunko, 1986), p. 308.

21. Frederik L. Schodt, "Manga: Submarine Metaphors," *Mainichi Daily News*, 29 February 1992, p. B9.

22. Ryuichi Nagao, "'Amerika no seiki' no makugire wa chikai" [The Curtain Is About to Come Down on the American Century], *Chuo Koron*, February 1991, pp. 80–93.

23. Donald M. Philippi, "Book Review: Gijutsu Bunmei no Hosoku, by Shuji Umano, Diamond Sha, 1984," *Technical Japanese Translation*, No. 19, p. 24; and Shuji Umano, *Gijutsu bunmei no hosoku* [Principles of a Technological Civilization] (Tokyo: Diamond-sha, 1984).

24. Shuji Umano, ed., *Bei CIA repooto "Japan 2000" no shinso wo eguru: tainichi sensen kyosho!*— *abakareta "akuma no sentaku"* [Rooting Out the Truth of the U.S. CIA "Report 2000": A Message of Declaration of War on Japan—The "Devil's Choice" Exposed] (Tokyo: Tokuma Shoten, 1992), p. 237.

25. Shuji Umano, *Jinrui bunmei hiho nippon* [Civilization Evolved from Japan], p. 224.

26. Laura King, "Japan-Jews," Associated Press Wire Service, 29 July 1993; and Jacob Morgan, *Saigo no kyoteki Nippon wo ute: yudaya sekai shihai no puroguramu* [Strike The Last Real Enemy, Japan: The Jewish Program for World Domination], Vols. 1–3, trans. Shotaro Oshino (Tokyo: Daiichi Kikaku Shuppan, 1993).

27. Hideo Levy, *Nihongo no shori* [Victory for the Japanese Language] (Tokyo: Kodansha, 1992), p. 216. (Quote translated by F. Schodt.)

28. "Gaikokujin haiseki bira demawaru" [Posters Calling for Expulsion of For-eigners Appear], *Asahi Shinbun* (evening edition), 7 April 1993, p. 27.

29. John G. Russel, *Nihonjin no kokujinkan: mondai wa "chibi-kuro sambo" dake de wa nai* [Japanese Views of Blacks: The Problem Isn't Just "Little Black Sambo"] (Tokyo: Shinpyosha, 1991), p. 43. (Quote translated by F. Schodt.)

30. Griffis, *The Romance of Conquest: The Story of American Expansion through Arms and Diplomacy* (Boston: W.A. Wilde, 1899), p. 17.

31. Griffis, *The Mikado's Empire*, p. 163.

32. "Uiiku endo keizai: Kasumigaseki chibeiha no yuutsu." [Weekend Econom-ics: Experts on U.S. at Kasumigaseki Are Depressed," *Asahi Shinbun*, 14 June 1992, p. 8.

33. Ibid.

34. Ibid.

35. "Watashi no Amerika" [My America], *Asahi Shinbun*, 9 November 1992, p. 17.

36. Ibid., 8 December 1992, p. 7.

37. Ryotaro Shiba, *Amerika sobyo* [Sketches of America] (Tokyo: Shincho Bunko, 1986), pp. 17–20.

38. Ibid., pp. 26–27, 388.

39. Haruo Motoazabu, "Motoazabu Haruo no tetsugakuteki DOS/V tooku (1)" [Haruo Motoazabu's Philosophical DOS/V talk (1)], *DOS/V Power*, April 1993, pp. 90–91.

40. Umano, *Jinrui bunmei hiho*, p. 222.

41. Lowell, *Soul of the Far East*, pp. 1–2.

BIBLIOGRAPHY

Agawa, Naoyuki. *Amerika ga kirai desuka* [Do You Hate America?]. Tokyo: Kodansha, 1993.

Barry, Dave. *Dave Barry Does Japan*. New York: Random House, 1992.

BenDasan, Isaiah. *Nihonjin to yudayajin* [The Japanese and the Jews]. Tokyo: Yamamoto Shoten, 1970.

Berh, Edward. *Hirohito: Behind the Myth*. New York: Villard Books, 1989.

Bessatsu rekishi dokuhon, Tokubetsu zokan 11: yudaya/nachis [Historical Reader, Special Supplement Edition No. 11: Jews/Nazis]. Tokyo: Shinjinbutsuoraisha, 1993.

Bessatsu Takarajima, ed. *Heisei gannen no uyoku* [The Right Wing in the First Year of Heisei]. Tokyo: JICC, 1989.

Bisland, Elizabeth, ed. *The Japanese Letters of Lafcadio Hearn*. Boston: Houghton Mifflin, 1910.

Brzezinski, Zbigniew. "Europe and Amerippon: Pillars of the Next World Order." *New Perspective Quarterly*, Spring 1990, pp. 18–19.

Chimoto, Hideki. *Tennosei no shinryakusekinin to sengo sekinin* [The Emperor System's Responsibility during the Invasion and in the Postwar Period. Tokyo: Aoki Shoten, 1990.

Choate, Pat. *Agents of Influence*. New York: Alfred A. Knopf, 1990.

Clinton, William J., and Albert Gore, Jr. *Technology for America's Economic Growth: A New Direction to Build Economic Strength*. 22 February 1993.

Cohen, Theodore. *Remaking Japan: The American Occupation as New Deal*. Edited by Herbert Passin. New York: Free Press, 1987.

Crichton, Michael. *Rising Sun*. New York: Ballantine Books, 1992.

Daniels, Roger. *The Politics of Prejudice: The Anti-Japanese Movement in California and the Struggle for Japanese Exclusion*. New York: Atheneum, 1968.

Dower, John W. *War Without Mercy: Race and Power in the Pacific War*. New York: Pantheon Books, 1986.

Dulles, Foster Rhea. *Yankees and Samurai: America's Role in the Emergence of Modern Japan, 1791–1900*. New York: Harper and Row, 1965.

Emmerson, John K. *A View From Yenan*. Washington, D.C.: Institute for the Study of Diplomacy, 1979.

Endo, Shusaku. *The Samurai*. Translated by Van C. Gessel. New York: Harper & Row, 1982.

Esthus, Raymond A. *Theodore Roosevelt and Japan*. Seattle: University of Washington Press, 1966.

Fallows, James. "Containing Japan." *Atlantic Monthly*, May 1989, pp. 40–54.

————, Chalmers Johnson, Clyde Prestowitz, and Karel van Wolferen. "Beyond Japan Bashing; The 'Gang of Four' Defends the Revisionist Line." *U.S. News and World Report*, 7 May 1990, pp. 54–55.

Fernandez-Armesto, Felipe. *Columbus*. Oxford: Oxford University Press, 1991.

Fielding, Norma. *In the Realm of a Dying Emperor*. New York: Vintage, 1993.

Friedman, George, and Meredith Lebard. *The Coming War with Japan*. New York: St. Martin's Press, 1991.

Graham, Edward M., and Paul Krugman. *Foreign Direct Investment in the United States*. Washington, D.C.: Institute for International Economics, 1989.

Grew, Joseph, C. *Ten Years in Japan: A Contemporary Record Drawn from the Diaries and Private and Official Papers of Joseph C. Grew, United States Ambassador to Japan, 1932–1942*. New York: Simon and Schuster, 1944.

Griffis, William Elliot. *The Mikado's Empire*. New York: Harper and Brothers Franklin Square, 1895.

————. *The Romance of Conquest: The Story of American Expansion through Arms and Diplomacy*. Boston: W. A. Wilde, 1899.

Harris, Townsend. *The Complete Journal of Townsend Harris; First American Consul General and Minister to Japan*. Garden City, New York: Doubleday, Dorand, 1930.

Hearn, Lafcadio. *Japan: An Attempt at Interpretation*. New York: MacMillan, 1904.

Heco, Joseph. Edited by James Murdoch. *The Narrative of a Japanese: What He Has Seen and the People He Has Met in the Course of the Last Forty Years*. Vol. 1, *From the Time of His Being Castaway in 1850 Down to the Fight of Shimonoseki*, and Vol. 2. San Francisco: American-Japanese Publishing Association [date unknown].

Heine, William. *With Perry to Japan; A Memoir by William Heine, Translated with an Introduction and Annotations by Frederic Trautmann*. Honolulu: University of Hawaii Press, 1990.

Hillenbrand, Barry. "America in the Mind of Japan." *Time*, 10 February 1992, pp. 20–23.

Ienaga, Saburo. *The Pacific War, 1931–1945: A Critical Perspective on Japan's Role in World War II*. New York: Pantheon Books, 1978.

Imai, Masaaki. *Kaizen (Ky'zen), the Key to Japan's Competitive Success*. New York: McGraw Hill, 1986.

Inose, Naoki. *Mikado no shozo* [Portrait of the Mikado]. Vols. 1 and 2. Tokyo: Shinchobunko, 1986.

Ishihara, Shintaro. *The Japan That Can Say No*. Translated by Frank Baldwin. New York: Simon and Schuster, 1989.

"Japan Survey." *The Economist*, 6 March 1993.

Jetro, ed. *U.S. and Japan in Figures, I & II*. Tokyo: Jetro, 1991–92.

Johnson, Chalmers. *MITI and the Japanese Miracle: The Growth of Industrial Policy, 1925–1975*. Stanford: Stanford University Press, 1982.

Kamata, Satoshi. *Kyoiku kojo no kodomotachi* [Children of Education Factories]. Tokyo: Kodansha Bunko, 1986.

———. *Toyota to Nissan: jodosha okoku no kurayami* [Toyota and Nissan: The Dark Side of the Auto Kingdom]. Tokyo: Kodansha Bunko, 1992.

Kaneko, Hisakazu. *Manjiro: The Man Who Discovered America*. Boston: Houghton Mifflin, 1956.

Kaplan, David E., and Alec Dubro. *Yakuza: The Explosive Account of Japan's Criminal Underworld*. New York: MacMillan, 1986

Katsuragi, Yoji. *Nihonjin ni natta Amerikajin gishi: Uiriamu Gohamu* [William Gorham: An American Engineer Who Became a Japanese]. Tokyo: Granpuri Shuppan, 1993.

Kawai, Kazuo. *Japan's American Interlude*. Chicago: University of Chicago Press, 1960.

Kawazumi, Tetsuo. *Nakahama Manjiro shusei* [The Manjiro Nakahama Collection]. Tokyo: Shogakukan, 1990.

Keizai Koho Center, ed. *Japan 1993: An International Comparison*. Tokyo: Keizao Koho Center, 1993.

Kenrick, Douglas Moore. *Where Communism Works: The Success of Competitive Communism in Japan*. Rutland, VT: Charles E. Tuttle, 1988.

Kodama, Sanehide. *American Poetry and Japanese Culture*. Hamden, Connecticut: Archon Books, 1984.

———, ed. *Ezra Pound and Japan: Letters and Essays*. Redding Ridge, Connecticut: Black Swan Books, 1987.

Kodansha Encyclopedia of Japan. Tokyo: Kodansha, 1983.

Komuro, Naoki. *Kokumin no tame no keizai genron II: Amerika gappei hen* [Economic Principles for the People, Part II: Incorporation with America]. Tokyo: Kobunsha, 1993.

Koren, Leonard. *283 Useful Ideas from Japan.* San Francisco: Chronicle Books, 1988.

Krugman, Paul. *The Age of Diminished Expectations: U.S. Economic Policy in the 1990s.* Cambridge: MIT Press, 1990.

————, ed. *Trade with Japan: Has the Door Opened Wider?* Chicago: University of Chicago Press, 1991.

Lazarus, David. "Base Price: U.S. Bases in Japan Face an Uncertain Future." *PHP Intersect,* October 1992, pp. 34–38.

Lea, Homer. *The Valor of Ignorance.* New York: Harper and Brothers, 1942.

Levy, Hideo. *Nihongo no shori* [Victory for the Japanese Language]. Tokyo: Kodansha, 1992.

Lewis, William S., and Naojiro Murakami, eds. *Ranald MacDonald: The Narrative of his early life on the Columbia under the Hudson's Bay Company's regime; of his experiences in the Pacific Whale Fishery; and of his great Adventure to Japan; with a sketch of his later life on the Western Frontier, 1824–1894.* Spokane: Eastern Washington State Historical Society, 1923.

Lowell, Percival. *The Soul of the Far East.* Boston: Houghton, Mifflin, 1888.

Lunde, Ken. *Understanding Japanese Information Processing.* Sebastopol, CA: O'Reilly and Associates, 1993.

Massarella, Derek. *A World Elsewhere: Europe's Encounter with Japan in the Sixteenth and Seventeenth Centuries.* New Haven: Yale University Press, 1990.

Miner, Earl. *The Japanese Tradition in British and American Literature.* Princeton: Princeton University Press, 1958.

Miyoshi, Masao. *As We Saw Them: The First Japanese Embassy to the United States (1860).* Berkeley: University of California Press, 1979.

Morita, Akio. "Shin-jiyu keizai e no teigen" [Proposal for a New Liberal Economy]. *Bungei Shunju,* February 1992, pp. 94–109.

Morrow, Lance. "Japan in the Mind of America." *Time.* 10 February 1992, pp. 16–20.

Nagao, Ryuichi. "'Amerika no seiki' no makugire wa chikai" [The Curtain Is About to Come Down on the American Century]. *Chuo Koron,* February 1991, pp. 80–93.

Nakane, Chie. *Japanese Society.* Berkeley: University of California Press, 1970.

Nakanishi, Akihiko, and Tatsumi Ito. "Seijika to yakuza no kenkyu" [A Study of Politicians and the Yakuza]. *Bungei Shunju.* January 1993, pp. 118–31.

Nitobe, Inazo. *The Works of Inazo Nitobe.* Vol. 4. Tokyo: University of Tokyo Press, 1972.

——— et al. *Western Influences in Modern Japan: A Series of Papers on Cultural Relations.* Chicago: University of Chicago Press, 1931.

———. Okimoto, Daniel I. *Between MITI and the Market: Japanese Industrial Policy for High Technology.* Stanford: Stanford University Press, 1989.

Parker, Jr., L. Craig. *The Japanese Police System Today: An American Perspective.* Tokyo: Kodansha International, 1984.

Perrin, Noel. *Giving up the Gun: Japan's Reversion to the Sword, 1543–1879.* Boston: Godine, 1979.

Plummer, Katherine. *The Shogun's Reluctant Ambassadors: Japanese Sea Drifters in the North Pacific.* Portland: Oregon Historical Society, 1991.

Polo, Marco. *The Book of Marco Polo* (copy with annotations by Christopher Columbus, which is conserved at the Capitular and Columbus Library of Sevilla). English translation of the publication by Juan Gil. Madrid: Testimonio, 1986.

Prestowitz, Jr., Clyde V. *Trading Places: How We Allowed Japan to Take the Lead.* New York: Basic Books, 1988.

Reischauer, Edwin O. *Japan: The Story of a Nation.* New York: Alfred A. Knopf, 1974.

Schodt, Frederik L. *Manga! Manga! The World of Japanese Comics.* Tokyo: Kodansha International, 1983.

———. *Inside the Robot Kingdom: Japan, Mechatronics, and the Coming Robotopia.* Tokyo: Kodansha International, 1988.

Sekai daihyakka jiten [Great World Encyclopedia]. Tokyo: Heibonsha, 1972.

Shiba, Ryotaro. *Amerika no sobyo* [Sketches of America]. Tokyo: Shincho Bunko, 1986.

Stevenson, Elizabeth. *Lafcadio Hearn.* New York: MacMillan, 1961.

Stevenson, Harold W., and James W. Stigler. *The Learning Gap: Why Our Schools are Failing and What We Can Learn from Japanese and Chinese Education.* New York: Summit Books, 1992

Thurow, Lester. *Head to Head: The Coming Economic Battle among Japan, Europe, and America.* New York: William Morrow, 1992.

Tyson, Laura D'Andrea. *Who's Bashing Whom? Trade Conflict in High-Technology Industries.* Washington, D.C.: Institute for International Economics, 1992.

Umano, Shuji, ed. *Bei CIA repooto "Japan 2000" no shinso wo eguru; tainichi sensen kyosho!— abakareta "akuma no sentaku"* [Rooting Out the Truth of the U.S. CIA "Report 2000": A Message of Declaration of War on Japan—The "Devil's Choice" Exposed]. Tokyo: Tokuma Shoten, 1992.

—-——. *Gijutsu bunmei no hosoku: 1990 nendai Nippon no joken* [Principles of a Technological Civilization: Requirements for Japan in the 1990s]. Tokyo: Diamond-sha, 1984.

—-——. *Jinrui bunmei hiho Nippon* [Civilization Evolved from Japan]. Tokyo: Tokuma Shoten, 1991.

Unger, J. Marshall. *The Fifth Generation Fallacy: Why Japan Is Betting Its Future on Artificial Intelligence.* New York: Oxford University Press, 1987.

Uno, Masami. *Kodai yudaya wa nippon ni fuin sareta* [Ancient Jewry Is Sealed in Japan]. Tokyo: Nippon Bungeisha, 1992.

Urabe, Toshio. *Fuajii Nippon to shin runessansu* [Fuzzy Japan and the New Renaissance]. Tokyo: Nihon Kyoiku Shinbunsha, 1990.

Vogel, Ezra. *Japan as Number One: Lessons for America.* New York: Harper and Row, 1979.

Westwood, J. N. *Russia against Japan, 1904–05: A New Look at the Russo-Japanese War.* Albany: State University of New York Press, 1986.

White, Theodore H. "The Danger from Japan." *New York Times Magazine*, 28 July 1985, p. 19.

Whiting, Robert. *You Gotta Have Wa.* New York: Macmillan, 1989.

Wiley, Peter Booth. With Korogi Ichiro. *Yankees in the Land of the Gods: Perry and the Opening of Japan.* New York: Viking, 1990.

Wolferen, Karel van. *The Enigma of Japanese Power: People and Politics in a Stateless Nation.* New York: Alfred A. Knopf, 1989.

Yamanouchi, Yoshio. "Yakuza wo nakushite wa ikenai wake" [Why the Yakuza Must Not Be Eliminated]. *Takarajima 30*, June 1993, pp. 130–38.

Yoshida, Ruiko. *Yoshida Ruiko no Amerika* [Ruiko Yoshida's America]. Tokyo: Kodansha Bunko, 1986.

Yoshimura, Akira. *Umi no sairei* [Celebration of the Sea]. Tokyo: Bunshun Bunko, 1989.

INDEX